This is a Man

"A study of Vladimir Putin and our modern era"

Jean-Paul Cassone'

Printed in U.S.A. for CSRV

(Cassone' Silk Road Ventures)

(JPC-book 2)

*(Master proof printed by CreateSpace, a DBA of On-Demand Publishing LLC)

*(Cover art by graphic artist Bonnie B. Brewer, Compass Printing, Saranac Lake, N.Y.)

Concerning the Author

A full detailed description about Jean-Paul Cassone' can be found within either his prior book Tandem "Escape to the multipolar world", or at Seeking Alpha at: http://seekingalpha.com/user/3843721/activity-feed#view=activity_feed

Some other aspects about the man which you won't find there are as follows. At the age of three he met Howard Hughes on the front steps of a country store style A&P that had sawdust on the floor in Bedford, New York. His family tree is diverse ranging from one of the most liberal Supreme Court Justices in its history to a U.S. Calvary general who served as the 7th president of the NRA. Though he is considered to be a casual Buddhist who frequented the more than 700 year old "Temple of Six Banyan Trees" in Guangzhou, China, the author's first 9 years of schooling were attended in the Roman Catholic school of St. Patrick's, under the instruction of The Sisters of Charity. He is the only non-Muslim former member of the Pakistani economic think tank Economistan and often kept company in the U.S. with various vice-presidents of finance in Merrill Lynch, Smith Barney and Aetna Life and Casualty, as well as the late Thomas E. Chandler, former editor to The Boston Herald Traveller.

During an intense three year stretch in Guangdong, China Jean-Paul Cassone' was an English instructor to more than 4,000 students for over 25 different organizations such as Nanhua University of Industry and Commerce, New Oriental School, China Com, English First, Alcanta, Guangdong University's minor school, Rockwell Automation, Total-Fina-Elf, Bank of China, 3 levels of kindergarten, every grammar school grade, every middle school grade, every high school grade and the first 3 years of college. He also served as a mock-IELTS examiner and taught English for several law firms, China Army Medical officers and casual adults. He was the very first person in S. China's educational history to successfully coordinate a "private industry entity" (in this case, a law firm) to come onto a China college campus and share insight with college students as to what might be expected of them in the private sector.

Mr. Cassone' also has a background in woman's fashions with both Polo Ralph Lauren, as well as for Fawbushs of Edina, MN and in the printing industry for FedEx Office-CPC, as well as for The Copy Factory of Palo Alto, CA. At this writing the author is on a prolonged writing sabbatical in the Adirondack Mountains of New York.

CSRV / staff writer

Table of Contents

"Far from learning from others' mistakes, we keep on repeating them"

Vladimir Putin

Chapter I

The Presidential Man

Though this book begins as a celebration of a very great man, Vladimir Putin, it is in no way meant to be misconstrued as a full-fledged biography. President Putin was chosen by me for this book's major theme, due purely to the fact that he is at the very top of the global charts, as a man who exemplifies possessing an authentic manhood not to mention, one to be emulated. To fully understand any man in today's world requires first to investigate under what set of circumstances that individual is being subjected to, as well as to explore the characteristics of his environment.

It is a sad day for Western culture when this President of the Russian Federation demonstrates more astute qualities to be an American president, over all the United States candidates for 2016 combined. While America's hyper-spiteful Zionist-Jewish press, along with the Bilderberger-Israeli, Globalist Banksters and Industrial Military Complex's power and wealth contraption insist on spinning and obliterating facts and truths at warp speed to abominate this man, President Vladimir Putin continues to stand tall. The unipolar friction erupts with a constant barrage of maliciously manufactured condemnations from its morally bankrupt and corrupt ideologist, trapped in the mudslides of their own gluttonous atrocities.

Western leadership has only succeeded to accomplish two things; expand Israel's interests and completely disgrace and dishonor its citizenry. When travelling the globe today it is now a shameful experience to be known as an American. It is high time for Americans who still possess a well preserved mind to give praise and respect to this man he has so ardently and strenuously earned. Western elites loathe President Putin for his dedicated patriotism and his Teflon resistance to "internationalism" and the selling of nations' souls to corporate interests, as well as far-flung experiments such as multiculturalism. The unipolar mongrels are appalled at this man's brilliant success of propagating such vigorous growth in Russian loyalty, pride, unity and a strengthened sense of confidence. So strong in fact that Crimeans voted 96% "yes" for rejoining back with Russia.

Russia's success in developing cohesive collaborations with such economic powerhouses as China, India, Brazil and Iran has given cause for a few popped veins in the neck of the New World Order beast. The BRIC nations' implementation of fresh alternatives to the IMF (International Monetary Fund) and the U.S. petrodollar are just additional magnetic trace elements to its appeal, which are isolating the West and sabotaging its fanatical and archaic need to dominate.

But there's something more directly unique about Vladimir Putin's own magnetism which he has portrayed so well and that is he has even sparked a strong following among Western citizens. This is largely due to the fact that he chooses to be himself and more importantly, to "be a man". A man with no shame, guilt or political correctness for living his natural, organic masculinity. This runs counter to the West's destabilizing kosher elitists who practice the desecration and erosion of sexual roles and role models in what was once a healthy society with a moral foundational fabric and an ethical backbone. In China white collar criminals oftentimes will face a firing squad and in Russia perhaps a lifetime in prison. However, in the Western nations of today it would not be an exaggeration to say that they are ruled by an elite criminality. In other words, Vladimir Putin exudes everything that America used to stand for.

The failure of multiculturalism is in its prohibition for white Europeans to demonstrate a self-identity, so it dilutes the culture ever so heavily towards its end goal of everyone becoming opaquely the same. It does not unify by assimilation, but rather it divides by abrasive polarization. A strong Christian Russia has their identity well intact and in Putin's Russia cultural problems are addressed organically from within the culture's originating countries and not through forced experimentation. Europe still has a remote chance of saving itself with Russia's help and improved relations. The "new and made worse" United States however, has lost its chance with Europe. They might make for colorful NATO photo ops, but upon a closer examination you will find every European cursing NATO under their breath. It is because Western citizens are now becoming increasingly aware that they are being bled to death by their very corrupt and programed politicians.

Vladimir Putin has displayed his honed skills not just on the global chessboard of geopolitics, but in the martial arts of judo. This requires a keen, pragmatic form of self-defense utilizing the leverage of an opponent's own weaknesses and force. This reflects a heightened degree of not just reflex dexterity and strength, but of composure, self-discipline, collectiveness and humility. He projects a slight resemblance and aura to that of a Renaissance man. This president permits himself to not only be humane but to reveal he's also quite capable of befriending anyone from a powerful nation to a baby bird.

On his worldly circuit this man Putin has not just rubbed elbows with heads-of-State, but silver screen legends like Steven Segal, Jean-Claude Van Damme and Leonardo De Caprio, as well as renowned chef Gordon Ramsey. What other nations' politicians might find too risky an embarrassing moment, this particular president demonstrates not only a wherewithal that rises to the occasion, but the savvy to land on his feet while making it all appear quite cool. These survival skills span an ever much broader spectrum, given the fact that this former low level KGB member is also a seasoned marksman, can commandeer a Russian bomber and skillfully ride a Harley Davidson home from work.

This all contrasts against a backdrop of a West, which at best once had a daddy Bush as president who, even though he was a former CIA director he would inevitably deliver a rather powdered milk version of being a bit of a klutz. And while daddy Bush openly proved to the world that he couldn't even shop his way out of a supermarket (he didn't know they used bar code scanners at the checkout) , or that his son wasn't known for much past raising a Dr. Pepper to his chin, Obama was stuck in the sand traps of your local golf course. As for this Russian president he has been sighted whipping his own car into local gas stations to pump his own gas while demonstrating he's also packed with the nerves of steel required to maneuver a Formula-1 race car at break-neck speeds. Being the natural man that he is, it's not unusual to see President Putin discussing important issues over a beer at the local tavern.

The president's focus on Russia's educational system has proven many positive results and his over-the-top delivery in implementing a flat-tax in Russia still has Western champions such as Steve Forbes doing cart wheels in the aisles. When once asked if he was the richest man in Russia he replied in a relaxed persuasion, "This is true. I am the richest person not only in Europe, but also in the world. I collect emotions and I am rich in that respect that the people of Russia have twice entrusted me leadership of such a great country as Russia. I consider this to be my biggest fortune. As for the rumors concerning my financial wealth, I have seen some pieces of paper regarding this. This is plain chatter, not worthy of discussion, plain bosh. They have picked this in their noses and have smeared this across their pieces of paper. This is how I view this".

Being known by many as perhaps the coolest president to ever make history, he also sports a love of wildlife and demonstrates a humane compassion not just for people, but animals as well. This all blends well in the sculpting of his complete male persona. He has avidly portrayed with videoed evidence, his comprehensive knowledge and awareness for the endangerment of species such as the polar bear and the Siberian tiger. The president-naturalist is spear-heading efforts toward actively rescuing the population of these animals and has proven to be a man of action.

Vladimir Putin himself often accompanies scientific crews to study these endangered species and is considered to be quite accurate with a tranquilizer gun. He once actually prevented a camera crew from a perilous, lethal fate. Being a man blessed with a finely-tuned sense of balance for whatever the occasion demands, from Rambo to Dr. Doolittle you can rest assured this man's actions will always be accurate and on-time.

Of course being his own manly self, he also has a world class appreciation for the female human species as well, when he's not busy visiting injured soldiers in hospitals, swimming with dolphins or hang-gliding with migratory birds. President Putin smartly never neglects keeping his physical health well-toned with his world class skills in his passion for skiing, horseback riding, hunting and fishing. Perhaps one of the most appealing characteristics to this

Renaissance man is that he is unaffected and unspoiled by their failed, liberal experiments which poisoned the male identity. He is his own person and a humane human being, deflecting any incoming arrows of guilt while organically and naturally living a manhood in the present tense. And it is these firm building blocks which are the footing to his foundational dexterity that enables him to be a world-class president and a genuine human being.

On July 15 and 16 of 2014 on the eve of a BRICS summit in Brazil, President Vladimir Putin offered an open interview to Russia's ITAR-TASS journalist:

Question: "The BRICS association, whose significance is increasing in the modern multipolar world, could advance important changes in international relations. What is the agenda and what plans do you as a Russian leader consider it important to discuss with your BRICS partners at the upcoming summit"?

President of Russia Vladimir Putin: "The modern world is indeed multipolar, complex and dynamic - this is objective reality. Any attempt to create a model of international relations where all decisions are made within a 'single pole' are ineffective, malfunction regularly and are ultimately set to fail".

"Those are the reasons why the interaction format proposed by Russia for such influential States such as the BRICS members has proven to be needed. Our joint efforts have truly contributed to enhancing predictability and sustainability in international relations".

"The forthcoming summit's theme is 'Inclusive Growth; Sustainable Solutions'. Therefore, we will consider the most urgent issues in global politics and the economy, as well as the BRICS development. I believe it is time to raise the BRICS' role to a new level and to make our association an unalienable part of the global management system for sustainable development. How can this be achieved in practice"?

"First of all, to develop cooperation in the U.N. in every possible way, persistently counteracting individual States' attempts to impose upon the international community the policies of displacing unwanted regimes and promoting unilateral solutions to crisis situations. We propose to create a mechanism of regular, high-level consultations between our foreign ministers on different regional conflicts to agree where possible, on common positions and joint efforts to ensure their political and diplomatic settlement".

"We should coordinate BRICS policy more actively and counteract security threats and challenges, including counter-terrorism. Among other ways this can be achieved is through the mechanism of counter-terrorism consultations. An important place on the agenda will be devoted to expanding cooperation to combat drug trafficking. We are ready to build up joint efforts to reinforce the international legal regime of drug control".

"Cooperation in setting rules of responsible behavior in global information space is another important issue. Such rules must be based on the principles of respect for a country's sovereignty, non-interference in domestic affairs, observance of human rights and freedom, as well as equal rights for all countries to participate in internet management. I think our joint efforts will ensure that the BRICS countries hold a leading position in strengthening international information security".

"We are planning to shape a joint information policy in the international arena to support BRICS' activity and to present a more unbiased picture of the world. Naturally we are going to thoroughly analyze the situation in the planet's hotspots. Those include Syria and Iraq, where the positions of extremist and terrorist groups are gaining strength. Serious attention should be given to the crisis in Ukraine and the international community's measures to stop the bloodshed in the southeast of this country".

"In the economic sphere, we are going to discuss the IMF reform. The BRICS countries are concerned about the unreasonable delay in holding debate on this subject. This jeopardizes all of the efforts of the G20 in this direction. In the meantime, it is the ease of fulfilling the rightful demands of the 'new economies' to balance the IMF according to the 21st century reality".

"One more important question we are going to raise at the summit is the increasing cases of unilateral sanctions. Recently Russia has been exposed to a sanction attack from the United States and its allies. We are grateful to our BRICS partners who have criticized such practices in different forms. At the same time, substantive conclusions should be drawn from the current situation. Together we should think about a system of measures that would help prevent the harassment of countries that do not agree with some foreign policy decisions made by the United States and their allies, but would promote a civilized dialogue on all points at issue based on mutual respect".

Question: "What progress has been made in realizing plans to develop economic interaction within the BRICS? Some time ago, there was talk about setting up the association's own bank; however, this initiative has not been realized yet. What are the prospects in this area? Do you believe it is possible for the BRICS countries to elaborate specific joint plans of action in response to different challenges"?

Vladimir Putin: "We intend to actively develop trade and economic ties within the association. The BRICS member countries share in Russian's foreign trade balance rising steadily; last year it has already reached 13.1%. Despite instability in the international economy, the volume of the BRICS countries' mutual trade is increasing (in 2013 it was over $300 billion). It is in our common interest to use the complementarity of national economies to the maximum. Cooperation opportunities are great indeed. This is the market with almost three billion consumers. The BRICS countries have unique natural resources and a substantial technological, financial and industrial potential".

"On Russia's initiative the BRICS' Economic Cooperation Strategy is being drafted at the moment. It will focus on creating preconditions for accelerated economic development and the strengthening of our international competitiveness in our countries, the expansion and diversification of trade relations and insuring interaction for innovative growth. A number of prospective cooperative ventures are being studied to make sure the document is backed by concrete investment projects. I will note that last year our countries' businesses established the BRICS Business Council. This institution is still to fully realize its potential, but we have already started work to identify and eliminate barriers that impede business interaction within the association".

"It is clear that all the BRICS economies need serious infrastructure modernization. Our initiative to establish the New Development Bank is aimed at expanding cooperation in this sphere. In the year since the Durban Summit, we have managed to achieve significant progress in this direction. In the near future we expect to finalize all the remaining issues and we will be able to use the Bank's potential to realize major projects in our own countries. Another important initiative that is underway is creating BRICS Contingent Reserve Arrangement. It will become a safety net to help us form a joint response to economic challenges".

"I would like to emphasize that both the New Development Bank and the Contingent Reserve Arrangement are practical steps for our countries, intended to strengthen international financial architecture and to make it more balanced and just. The BRICS countries have shared attitudes towards other modern challenges in the economy, including the prompt completion of the Doha Round Negotiations, creating a more just global trade system and ensuring transparency in regional trade agreements".

Question: "How solid can a union of countries be if the majority of them do not have common borders? Is it possible that global processes will lead to the situation when over time, the cooperation between the member countries dies out, as it sometimes happens with regional associations? Are there any plans to reinforce a political element in BRICS and add a military aspect to these countries' interaction"?

Vladimir Putin: "In the modern world the factor of common borders does not play a role. On the contrary, global processes encourage us to join efforts as challenges and problems become shared. In the BRICS case we see a whole set of coinciding strategic interests. First of all this is the common intention to reform the international monetary and financial system. In the present form it is unjust to the BRICS and to the new economies in general. We should take a more active part in the IMF and World Banks' decision-making system. The international monetary system itself depends a lot on the U.S. dollar or to be precise, on the monetary and financial policy of the U.S. authorities. The BRICS countries want to change this".

"Another long-term common interest of the association's members is strengthening the rule of international law and the U.N.'s leading role in the international system. To be honest, without Russia's and China's principled position on Syria in the Security Council the events in that country would have followed the Libyan and Iraq scenario. Certainly the BRICS countries intend to strengthen the political element of our cooperation. That is why we will develop the practice of mutual consultations and joint actions in international organizations first of all, in the U.N. In the long term we will create a vertical BRICS secretariat. At the same time I would like to stress that we do not have any plans to form a BRICS military and political alliance".

The president came from an ordinary, yet special family. He was born October 7th, 1952 in Leningrad. Vladimir Putin recalled, "I come from an ordinary family and this is how I lived for a long time nearly my whole life. I lived as an average, normal person and I have always maintained that connection. We lived simply – cabbage soup, cutlets, pancakes, but on Sundays and holidays my Mom would bake very delicious stuffed buns (pirozhki) with cabbage, meat and rice and curd tarts (tatrushki)". Though his mother's approval of his passion for judo came rather slowly, it was finally accepted. "Every time I went to practice session she would grumble, "He's off to his fights again". His coach later visited his parents and after relaying their son's skills and accomplishments, his family disposition towards the sport changed.

"My father (Vladimir Putin) was born in St. Petersburg in 1911. When World War I began, life in St. Petersburg became hard. People were starving, so the entire family moved to Pominovo, a village in the Tver Region my grandmother came from. Incidentally, my relatives still vacation in the houses where my grandparents lived. It was in Pominovo that my father met my mother and they got married at the age of 17".

His father was active in the war. Later, in the 1950's he was employed as a security guard and eventually, as a foreman of a carriage works. The Putin family found themselves moving once again, after the war. It was a room in a communal apartment (kommunalka), in a usual St. Petersburg structured house on Baskov Lane. President Putin recalled, "It was a building with a well-liked yard, fifth floor, no elevator. Before the war (World War II), my parents occupied half of the house in Peterhof and we were very proud of the living standards they had achieved then. It wasn't really much, but it seemed like an ultimate dream to them".

During the 1960's, Vladimir Putin attended Primary School No. 193 in Leningrad. Following the eighth grade he attended a chemistry magnet school, High School No. 281 under the authority of a technology institute and completing his studies in 1970. "I was always late for my first class," Putin recalls. "So even in the Winter I didn't have time to dress properly."

During his grade school years at No. 193 in Leningrad Vladimir Putin can remember he was more of a troublemaker than a Pioneer. One of his teachers Vera Gurevich recalls, "In the fifth grade he hadn't yet found himself, but I could feel the potential, the energy and the character in him. I saw that he had a great deal of interest in language; he picked it up easily. He had a very good memory and an agile mind. I thought, something good will come of this boy, so I decided to give him more attention, to distract him from the boys on the street".

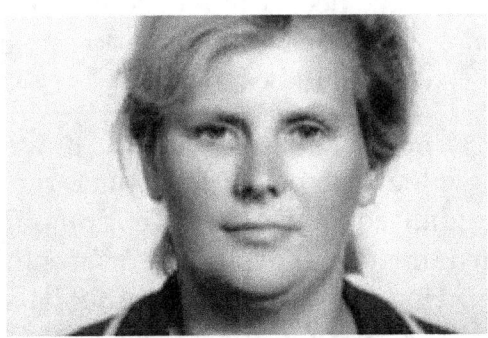

Until grade six, he was not very interested in studying, but Ms. Gurevich saw that he could get higher grades. So she met with his father, asking him to perhaps make attempts to persuade his son.

Though it didn't seem to help much, Vladimir Putin did eventually experience a noticeable change in his approach towards his studies during the sixth grade time period. He himself admits, "Other priorities were emerging. I was asserting myself through sports, achieving something. There were new goals too. No doubt, this had an enormous effect".

It was during the sixth grade that Vladimir Putin decided he needed to achieve something in life. He later found that this came rather easy to him and it wasn't long before he was inducted into the Pioneers organization. Once there he swiftly rose to become head of a detachment in his Pioneer class. "It became clear that street smarts were not enough, so I began doing sports. But even that was not enough for maintaining my status so to speak, for very long. I realized that I also needed to study well," Putin said.

Vladimir Putin became a student of law in 1970 at the Leningrad State University. In 1975 he earned his degree and during the late 1970's and early 1980's he studied at KGB School No. 1 at Moscow.

The president confided, "Even before I finished high school I wanted to work in intelligence. Granted, soon after I decided I wanted to be a sailor, but then I wanted to do intelligence again. In the very beginning I wanted to be a pilot".

And so it was that even before Vladimir Putin was out of school, he felt an evident magnetic tug towards the intelligence profession. So he inquired to a public reception office of the KGB Directorate to learn the formal protocols for becoming an intelligence officer. He was informed he would have two options; either serve in the army first, or finish college. For the scholastic option he was told that having a law degree would be an advantage. "And from that moment I began preparing myself to enter the law department at Leningrad State University," he stated.

In 1970 he was admitted into the university's law department. "We had a class of 100 people and only 10 of them entered immediately after high school. The rest had already completed military service. So for us the high school graduates, only one out of forty was admitted. I got four out of five for the essay, but top marks for everything else, so I passed," the president quipped. "When I began studying at the university, new goals and new values emerged. I mainly focused on studies and began seeing sports as a secondary. But of course, I trained on a regular basis and participated in nationwide competitions, almost out of habit".

Upon graduating from the university, Vladimir Putin was assigned to work in the State security agencies. "My personal perception of the KGB was based on the idealistic stories I had heard about in intelligence". Putin the intern was appointed to the Directorate Secretariat and then the counterintelligence division for about a five month hitch. Six months later he was in operations personnel retaining courses.

The president then spent, yet another six months working in the counterintelligence division. It was here that he caught the attention of foreign intelligence officers. "Fairly quickly, I left for special training in Moscow, where I spent a year. Then I returned again to Leningrad, worked there for the First Main Directorate –

the intelligence service. That directorate had branches in major cities of the Soviet Union, including Leningrad. I worked there for about four and a half years".

Mr. Putin then returned to Moscow again, only this time to study at the Andropov Red Banner Institute and was trained for a trip to Germany. Upon completion of his studies at the Andropov Institute he departed for East Germany in 1985 and worked there until 1990. However, before his departure another major event took shape in Mr. Putin's life; "romance" for keeps. It was through a mutual friend he met Lyudmila Shkrebneva. Lyudmila had come with a friend to Leningrad for three days, working as a flight attendant on domestic airlines. "I was already working in the First Main Directorate in St. Petersburg, when a friend of mine called and invited me to the Arkady Raikin theatre. He said he already had tickets and mentioned there would be two young ladies joining us. So we went to the performance and the young ladies did join us. The next day we went to the theatre again, but it was now my turn to buy tickets. And the same thing happened on the third day. I then began dating one of the girls. I became friends with Lyudmila, my future wife," Vladimir Putin reflected.

"There was something about Vladimir that attracted me. Three or four months later, I already knew this was the man I needed," Lyudmila recalled. Three years after their first meeting Vladimir proposed to Lyudmila. "I knew that if I did not marry for another two or three years, I would not marry at all. True, I was used to life as a bachelor, but Lyudmila changed that," the president admits. They were married on July 28, 1983.

Before their departure to Germany, in 1985 Vladimir and Lyudmila Putin received their first daughter, Maria. Katerina their second daughter, was born in 1986, in Dresden. Both girls were named in honor of their grandmothers, Maria Putin and Yekaterina Shkrebneva. Lyudmila informed, "Vladimir loves his daughters very much. Not all fathers are as loving with their children as he is. And he has always spoiled them, while I was the one who had to discipline them," she recalls.

Putin served at the local intelligence office in Dresden, East Germany from 1985 – 1990. During the tenure of his service, he was promoted to Lieutenant Colonel and senior assistant to the head of the department. He was awarded the Bronze Medal during 1989 in the German Democratic Republic, for "Faithful Service to the National People's Army". Mr. Putin mentioned, "My work was going well. It was a normal thing to be promoted just once while working abroad. I was promoted twice".

In 1990, Vladimir Putin returned from Germany, to Leningrad and became the Assistant Rector of the State University there. His political career began to blossom in 1996 and he and his family moved to Moscow. While still in Leningrad Mr. Putin recalls, "I was happy to find work at Leningrad State University. I took the job hoping at the same time to write my Ph.D. thesis and perhaps stay on and work afterwards. That was how I ended up in 1990, becoming assistant to the rector in charge of international relations".

While in Leningrad he also was an advisor to the chairman of the Leningrad City Council. Beginning in June of 1991 he was Chairman of the Committee for International Relations at St. Petersburg City Hall. From 1994 onward, he simultaneously served as Deputy Chairman of the St. Petersburg City Government. It was during the president's career at City Hall that he submitted his resignation to the KGB.

Having moved with his family to Moscow in 1996, Vladimir Putin was offered the Deputy Chief post of the Presidential Property Management Directorate. He recalls, "I would not say I did not like Moscow, but simply that I liked St. Petersburg more. But Moscow was very obviously a European city". His career rise grew rapidly and in March of 1997 he was appointed Deputy Chief of Staff of the Presidential Executive Office and Chief of Main Control Directorate. Vladimir Putin conducted the demands of this challenging itinerary with herculean execution, as he still reserved the time to defend a doctorate thesis on economics at the St. Petersburg State Mining Institute. It all paid-off handsomely as immediately following this moment in time, Mr. Putin's career seemed to catapult at a mach-5, breakneck speed.

By May of 1998 he is made First Deputy Chief of Staff of the Presidential Executive Office. During the following month he was then appointed Director of the Federal Security Service and in a whirlwind fashion he landed firmly on his feet by March 1999 to achieve the position of Secretary of the Security Council of the Russian Federation. Perhaps just when you thought you've caught your breath in keeping up with this man's zenith-streak of professionalism, there is yet more. Came the month of August in 1999, Vladimir Putin is appointed Prime Minister of the Russian Government, a post offered to him by the then sitting president Boris Yeltsen.

Mr. Putin recalled later on, "Mr. Yeltsen invited me to come and see him and he said that he wanted to offer me the prime minister's job. Incidentally, he never used the word 'successor' in his conversation with me then, but spoke of becoming prime minister with prospects; and said that if all went well, he thought this could be possible". Vladimir Putin's term spent in the prime minister's office is described by him as being both an honor and an interesting experience. "I thought then, if I can get through a year that will already be a good start. If I can do something to help save Russia from falling apart then this would be something to be proud of". Then suddenly, beyond any aspiring, upward-mobile politician's wildest dream, shortly before the 2000th New Year arrived, the President of Russia, Boris Yeltsen proposed that Vladimir Putin become acting President.

"Two or three weeks before New Year, Mr. Yeltsen called me to his office and he said he had decided to step down. This meant I would have to become Acting President," Mr. Putin shared. He describes this as being a most difficult decision, given the position at that particular moment was, "a rather heavy load to bear". "I had my own thoughts, my own reasoning, but at the same time there was another logic I had to consider too. Fate was offering me a chance to work for the country at the very highest level and it would have been foolish to say, 'no, I'm going to go sell sunflower seeds instead,' or 'go into private legal practice'. I could do all those other things later, after all and so I decided this had to come first and everything else later," Putin confides. And so on December 31, 1999, Vladimir Putin became Acting President of the Russian Federation.

On March 26, 2000, Vladimir Putin was elected President of Russia. Following this term he was re-elected to a second term on March 14, 2004. By Presidential Executive Order he was appointed Prime Minister on May 8, 2008. During his very first inauguration speech, President Putin states, "We have common aims, we want our Russia to be a free, prosperous, flourishing, strong and civilized country. A country its citizens are proud of and that is respected internationally". In addition, he announced that he would be guided by the interests of the State. "Perhaps it will not be possible to avoid mistakes, but what I can promise and what I do promise is that I will work openly and honestly".

Concurrent to his inauguration speech, throughout the time that follows and including this very minute, Vladimir Putin has also stood by his words which follow: "I consider it to be my sacred duty to unify the people of Russia, to rally citizens around clear aims and tasks and to remember every day and every minute that we have one Motherland, one people and one future".

On March 14, 2004 Vladimir Putin was re-elected to his second term. On May 26, 2004 he addressed the Federal Assembly with these words, "Our goals are very clear. We want high living standards and a safe, free and comfortable life for the country. We want a mature democracy and a developed, civil society. We want to strengthen Russia's place in the world. But our goal, I repeat, is to bring about a noticeable rise in our people's prosperity".

President Putin was appointed Russian Prime Minister on May 8, 2008 by Presidential Executive Order. At a session of the Russian Federation State Duma Putin stated, "Russia has grown much stronger in recent years. We have enough resources to tackle still more ambitious tasks and goals. The important thing is to make competent, effective and proper use of the accumulated potential. For my part I am ready to exert every effort to achieve the goals set, to deliver new and significant results for the prosperity of our country and for the sake of a worthy life for Russian citizens".

"People" were always at the center of the Prime Minister's attention. Putin himself had said that the authorities must draw their support solely from the Russian people and that if this support was absent, the authorities would have no place in power. Putin was nominated as candidate for Russian President in November 2011. It was in the summer of 2010 that he took the reconstruction of homes and compensation for victims of wildfires, under his personal control. At the sites where reconstruction for these victims took effect, around-the-clock monitoring systems were set-up. The sites were also equipped with video cameras rolling 24/7. This enabled all construction work to be monitored at three separate locations; the Government's website, Vladimir Putin's personal residence and from The Government House itself.

One million rubles ($33,000) in compensation was awarded to families of those killed by the fires. In addition, each family member affected by the fires each received 100,000 rubles. A total of 2,200 families received new built homes and by the start of the following winter, all others affected either received new apartments or compensation. Mr. Putin stated, "If I do something I try to see it through to its completion, or at least try to ensure that it brings the maximum result".

On the commodities front Vladimir Putin has been a man of action as well. "Step by step we are becoming full-fledged masters of our own food and agricultural markets. This is the result of our work to develop the country's agricultural sector and is the visible fruit of the hard work put in by our grain growers, livestock farmers and processing companies," Mr. Putin said.

Another priority for the president was his support for the military servicemen and women. By 2013 not only did they see major increases to their income and pensions, but their housing as well. Vladimir Putin announced on September 5, 2011 that teacher's wages nation-wide increased and was made equally fair and in keeping with all other regions, over the course of the 2011-2012 academic year. He was seen as actively participating in this process personally.

For one to better comprehend this man Putin, it is necessary to become better familiarized with the shape of the world and global events taking place during his challenging climb to success. While President Putin was busy "raising" his people's standards of living, by the end of 2011 Americans' median income actually became lower than it was ten years prior. Lower than at any point since 1996, in fact.

To lend evidence to just how much the U.S. economy has been moving in the opposite direction of Russia's, since 1987 Americans' median incomes have "completely decoupled" downward from the ascension of productivity, private employment and real GDP, at an ever greater and widening gap. The wisdom of both the Russian Federation and its BRICS sister-State China, in comparison to the U.S. is quite an obvious contrast to observe. For one, these are just some of the things which both Russia and China do "not" subject their citizenry to, which America does inflict upon its workforce:

- damaging tax policies
- damaging trade policies
- malicious globalization practices
- the offshoring of jobs
- mismanaging technology

Both China and Russia have so far, clearly demonstrated that they favor their people over profits and technology. This is where America is quickly losing its appeal, by openly permitting its people to become "disposable" and to be handled like trash. The multipolar wisdom of BRICS nations is that when it comes to one machine replacing fifteen or twenty workers, they will leave the workers, they will not use that machine in instances that will leave workers destitute, with no alternatives and homeless.

I personally witnessed this while living several years in China's Guangdong Province. I observed construction of a 10 to 12 story building that was being completely done by hand, mortar and all. Yes they had the machines that would pump the cement up from a truck, just like the U.S., but instead they permitted many workers to hand wheel it from mixers on the constructing floors. In another example, China has the technology and machines to sweep the city streets, but instead they allow a small army of women with commercial size brooms to perform the task.

The same went for demolitions. I watched an army of 40 men with long handled sledge hammers completely demolish and take down a five story building slated for removal. The monies the machines save has the potential to actually worsen the economy, benefitting only a very few, when mismanaged by present day American standards and not of the Russian and/or Chinese approach to management.

Technology is "a tool". If used wisely it can be utilized as leverage to greatly benefit all. But if it is not managed and controlled properly, it has the potential to overtake all involved. Thus far President Putin's wisdom has prevailed over the West in not just managing technology, but in managing change. America has fallen ever deeper by unleashing technology without a cautious adherence to a specific set of standards and regulations to effectively raise "everyone's" prosperity.

America's employers are falling victim to purchasing more technology over hiring more workers. This creates a preference to capital over labor. These practices in turn, puts into motion a spiraling, downward effect in both wages and job creation opportunities.

What's startling about the displacement of workers from technology is that it does not only affect a menial workforce. Many high-skilled, high-wage jobs such as translations and legal research are also falling victim. Vladimir Putin has thus far, wisely averted this pitfall for his nation's people, which the U.S. is evermore falling into, unabated. Given its present course, America is riding a runaway train and before its final collision, we will find there is a nation ruled by computers and robots over a segment of humanity that will become ever more beholden to it for basic foods and shelter, where the dominant percentage of the population will be the unemployed.

President Vladimir Putin couldn't have picked a better time in history to be president, although I will confess whoever is his successor in say 20 years from now, will surely have a much less intense and challenging time with it. What I am trying to credit him with is the fact that "he rose to the occasion" and took ownership of his position at a moment in history when very few would have even dared to try. And it is directly related to the fact that he is "a man of his word" when he said, "If I do something, I try to see it through to its completion". It is now a shear fact that Russia's rise has been pushed into a continuum, compounding an ever impressionable sense of a nation that beams with a pride of great substance and an ever-trending, global example of a very wise, healthy, strong, enduring and compassionate leadership, unmatched in stamina and forever beholden to one man who cares very much, Vladimir Putin.

Other conditions affecting the environment under which Mr. Putin has been forced to work under, are the aspects and nature of global finance. The World Bank has predicted the U.S. dollar is soon to lose its dominance. "Multipolar" correlates into "multi-currency" and the world's financial system is racing towards making this a prominent standard practice in less than a decade. Mansoor Dailami, an expert from the World Bank and co-author of the report, "Global Development Horizon's Multipolarity: The New Global Economy" states as follows, "Over the next decade the influence of the Yuan will continue to grow thanks to the growth of the Chinese economy, as well as the expansion of the Chinese banks and corporations into the global market".

A World Bank forecast also predicts the six leading emerging economies of Brazil, China, India, Indonesia, South Korea and Russia will provide over half of the increase in the world's GDP during the next 8 to 10 years. Chief Economist from the World Bank, Justin Yifi Lin sees a gradual shift in the poles of the world economy, shifting in the direction of these six countries. He predicts their external financial flows shall allow poor and developing countries to lift their GDPs as well. However, it is my prediction that the developed economies of Japan, the UK and U.S. will be "flat to negative" during these next ten years. Why? Simply put, they are streaming towards becoming "the new third world countries of the future" due plainly to the fact that they have been ruled by criminals whose citizens chose to ignore and not question.

Surprisingly (with much thanks to Vladimir Putin), the Russian ruble is now being touted among financial experts as one of their recommended alternative currencies to the U.S. dollar. Chief economist for Deutsche Bank in Yaroslav Lissovolik, Russia, Rossiyskaya Gazeta states, "I believe that one can hardly speak about the monopoly of the U.S. dollar any longer, because the defacto currency system relies heavily on the euro, the yen and other currencies. Of course the role the U.S. dollar and euro, from my point of view will be reduced. Against this backdrop, I think not only the Chinese yuan, but the Russian ruble may strengthen its position as a reserve currency. In general, multi-currency system will reflect the weight of the developing countries in the world economy that will grow quite rapidly over the next several decades. The growth rates in the developing countries will be higher than that of some leaders of the developed world, such as the U.S. and Europe".

It should be noted that the World Bank report had been issued when the United States had reached its national debt limit, set by law, of $14.3 trillion. Gazeta also added, "..., I believe that Russia has an opportunity to strengthen the position of the ruble to become the world's reserve currency".

Another integral part of the global reality President Putin inherited to his challenges is the West turned on its head. Given the fact that the U.S. has now gained a psychotic reputation of being the world's leading pathological liar, with Europe as its lap dog. Since the Warsaw Pact disbanded in 1991, any intelligent bystanders walk away scratching their heads as to why America's embarrassing and outdated anti-Russian NATO is still trying to get an erection! The shear bigotry it assumes produces nothing more beyond a shameful disgrace as a "hate tank". It no longer serves any purpose beyond lining the pockets of elitist armament dealers who are too over weighted in the investments of warmongering and death. It is an obstacle to all progress and it is "reverse-evolution" and pro-Neanderthal which cannot be packaged any other way than as a deliberate destabilization plan of a tried and failed system in unipolarism.

Much in the style of the way U.S. President Kennedy's death was projected, U.S. bloody coups are now propagandized as "democratic revolutions". NATO's expansion is increasingly guilty of numerous violations in international law and commitments made during Germany's reunification. This demonstrates the West to currently be governed by very reckless and criminal individuals who have completely uncoupled from the consensus of the free world's majority, as well as the majority of its own people. This makes both the U.S. and NATO walking violations to their own core ideals. To proclaim to uphold democracy while demonstrating nothing other than totalitarianism is "fascism", not democracy.

Investigative historian Eric Zuesse puts it in perspective eloquently; "Europe's remaining allied with the U.S. and participating in NATO, especially after having been instructed by America to lie and to deceive Gorbachev (George H.W. Bush) who behaved honorably, is Europe's great shame. A truth is Russia's case. The U.S. is in fact, Europe's enemy – not merely Russia's enemy. Not merely the truth's enemy. Not merely democracy's enemy".

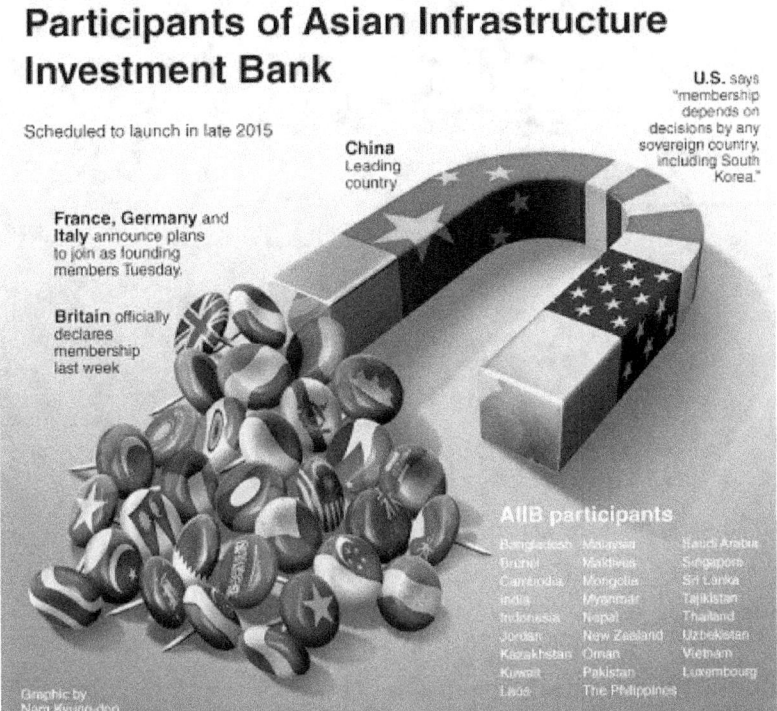

Participants of Asian Infrastructure Investment Bank

Scheduled to launch in late 2015

China
Leading
country

U.S. says
"membership
depends on
decisions by any
sovereign country,
including South
Korea."

France, Germany and
Italy announce plans
to join as founding
members Tuesday.

Britain officially
declares
membership
last week

AIIB participants

Bangladesh	Malaysia	Saudi Arabia
Brunei	Maldives	Singapore
Cambodia	Mongolia	Sri Lanka
India	Myanmar	Tajikistan
Indonesia	Nepal	Thailand
Jordan	New Zealand	Uzbekistan
Kazakhstan	Oman	Vietnam
Kuwait	Pakistan	Luxembourg
Laos	The Philippines	

Graphic by
Nam Kyung-don

The unipolar West has been sent into a panic. U.S.-Israeli –
Turkish led terrorists conducting stolen oil operations through
Syria bears evidence enough. Having already been pushed out of
Asia by China, the West is suffering immeasurably as President
Putin and the world dismantle this unipolar disorder, piece by
piece, region by region, as well it should be. For as all the world is
witnessing, America and its NATO club members have now strayed
so far from the roots of their founding ideals, to the extremes of
actively participating in State-sponsored terrorism. This now
exposes a very diseased elite within their apparatus, as being the
true cause of all terrorism from its onset.

Like an intoxicated poker player the unipolar world sits at the table, playing its last remaining strategy. Being now out of gold, out of money and up to its eyeballs in debt, it resorts pathetically and maliciously to false-flags, lying, cheating and making flagrant provocations to instigate war. Yet this is a small percentage of the tumultuous conditions under which the leaders of a sane world, such as President Putin's Russia, have been forced to conduct themselves under. Blatant disinformation of the truth has blanketed the unipolar's citizenry.

However, sometimes the truth is manifested regardless. Take for instance the U.S. Congresswoman Tulsi Gabbard, who herself did two tours of duty in Iraq. She calls Washington's efforts "counterproductive" and "illegal" and accused the CIA of arming terrorists the White House calls "America's sworn enemies". This House Democrat actually joined with one of her political rivals, Republican Adam Scott to co-sponsor a Bill to what they termed, "Stop the Illegal War to Overthrow Assad". While President Putin has worked vigorously to uplift Russia's living standards, the Israeli colony America, now continuously lowers theirs through wasteful funding of creating its own enemies, which it trains and arms. This is truly an Industrial Military Complex gone berserk!

In another example of Western desperation, we have them seen "silencing the truth in media", a supposed birthright to being an American. During this past 2015 the West has experienced a virtual blackout of news surrounding the seventh annual BRICS Summit in Ufa, Russia. The mainstream media in the U.S. (ABC, CBS, NBC, and CNN), which is highly Zionist controlled from top management on down, has not only refused to cover this historic event, but failed to give any explanation as to why! This has sentenced the majority of Americans to be deprived of any factual events concerning this powerful coalition of nations, which have put into place an alternative system that will greatly reduce U.S. influence in the world and pull the plug on its superpower antics.

The wisdom of the BRICS nations' leadership (Brazil, Russia, India, China and South Africa) is well aware that global security cannot be entrusted to a country which see's war and sponsoring terrorists as an acceptable form of geopolitical behavior. They realize the U.S. today for what it truly has become; an obstacle in sharing global financial power. As mentioned in my prior book, "Tandem" the nations of the multipolar world have chosen to create a parallel monetary system which better serves them. The brilliance of Vladimir Putin has greatly inspired this process throughout, in fact it would have no soul if it weren't for this great man. He was the first to see that what the multipolar world needed was to construct its own system in order to cease to be made indispensable. He realized too that they needed to enable themselves to utilize their own currencies and issue their own funding, while attracting investors for its many projects in an upbeat environment with visible oversight, free from covert political corruption.

On July 9th, 2015 President Putin announced that the BRICS New Development Bank would become fully operational, financing energy projects in 2016. It will also finance large-scale transport projects and industrial development. President Putin is actively involved in Russia's blueprint for mapping the BRICS investment cooperation. The new $100 billion international bank opened in Shanghai, China during July of 2015. The bank's prospects are bright as it continues to accept new members. Argentina, Mexico, Nigeria, Indonesia as well as others, have already announced their eagerness to join.

Associate Professor Roman Andreeschev, at the Department for Foreign Area Studies and International cooperation at the Institute of Public Administration and Management clearly stated, "BRICS members have been emphasizing the need to reform the IMF since 2009, so that the developed countries could have a more equitable system of governance in international financial institutions. This idea found support at the G20 in 2009. If we look at the BRICS meeting in Fortaleza of 2014 we will see the declaration mentions not only reform of the financial system, but also of the U.N. Security Council, the U.N. itself and the World Bank. That is, we see that the ambitions and aspiration of developing countries, the BRICS countries, have been growing".

"If you look at the APEC summit that was held in Beijing 2015, or at the G20 summit in Brisbane, Australia, then it becomes clear that the main question was about the construction of infrastructure to help businesses increase turnover. Therefore, the participation of State structures in the implementation of infrastructure projects is an issue of first priority", says Andreeschev. The Director of the Analytical Department of Nord-Capital, Vladimir Rozhankovsky told Pravda News, "I do not think it (the BRICS New Development

Bank) will be big competition for the IMF, as the IMF as a rule, does not finance structural projects. The IMF is a sovereign structure. The IMF as we know, comes to the rescue when the entire financial system of this or that country is standing on the verge of collapse of great difficulties. Yet, the new banks of the BRICS countries will be a good replacement to the International Bank for Reconstruction and Development (IBRD), the activity of which died away during recent years".

However, getting back to Professor Andreeschev's interpretation, he believes the BRICS New Development Bank will be a significant player in international finance, as well as a serious contender to both the World Bank and the IBRD. It will not only be in direct competition of their interests, but put an end to their formerly rigged terms and take-it-or-leave-it attitudes in agreements.

To promote bilateral trade and investment Russia and China have agreed to utilize each other's currencies, with President Putin mentioning that Russia would be keen to expand the use of national currencies with other BRICS countries. The president stated, "I think that such development with India, Brazil and South Africa would be interesting and could no doubt, lift the level of turnover. A pool of nominal currency reserves, with capital of $100 billion will give us an opportunity to react to financial market fluctuations, in a timely and appropriate manner".

The New Development Bank's website now more specifically describes itself as "an alternative to the existing U.S.-dominated World Bank and International Monetary Fund (IMF)", addressing the needs of infrastructure and sustainable development. In the words of geopolitical writer Mike Whitney, contributor to "Hopeless: Barrack Obama and the Politics of Illusion" (Ak Press), "The dollar is toast, the IMF is toast. The institutions that support U.S. power are crumbling before our very eyes. The BRICS have had enough; enough war, enough Wall Street, enough meddling and hypocrisy and austerity and lecturing. This is farewell. Sure it will take time, but Ufa marks a fundamental change in thinking, a fundamental change in approach and a fundamental change in strategic orientation. The BRICS are not coming back, they're gone for good, just as Washington's 'pivot to Asia' is gone for good. There's just too much resistance. Washington has simply overplayed its hand, worn out its welcome. People are sick of us. Can you blame them"?

The BRICS New Development Bank (NDB) is blossoming its first bud as Beijing is already underway in setting up a cousin to the NDB, a separate "Asian Infrastructure Investment Bank" (AIIB), as it seeks a broader role geopolitically to reflect its ascension in becoming the world's second-largest economy. Chinese Finance Minister Lou Jiwei, addressed the questions of competition into a much clearer focus, "The NDB will supplement the existing international financial system in a healthy way and explore innovations in governance models".

The launch of the NDB came just two weeks following the BRICS summit hosted by Vladimir Putin. After suffering huge currency fluctuations and a struggle in attracting new investors, after the West sponsored the "illegal" Ukrainian coup, Moscow can now safely rely upon the NDB and BRICS currency reserves as a more dependable, alternative global financial resource. At the time of the most recent summit, Russian Foreign Minister Sergey Lavrov mentioned in a statement that BRICS "..., illustrates a new polycentric system of international relations, demonstrating the increasing influence of new centers of power". This brings a much needed sense of "financial order" to the geopolitical arena.

The Asia Development Bank (ADB), a regionally focused financial institution has announced, it too will be looking forward to working with the NDB. That the BRICS bank would aim to challenge alternative, unipolar agencies is flatly denied by Chinese analysts. Li Daxiao, Chief Economist for Yingda Securities stated, "It's a compliment instead of a challenge, to exiting international institutions. It can help strengthen the currency markets and maintain a stable financial order through the internal stabilization of the BRICS countries".

The China-based Asian Infrastructure Investment Bank (AIIB) will be headquartered in Beijing with China being the largest shareholder at 30%. Its legal framework was signed during June of 2015 by 50 founding member countries. Major Asian and European economies such as Australia, France, the UK and Germany have joined the AIIB. The world's largest and third largest economies, the U.S. and Japan have foolishly declined to do so. It is my conservative conclusion, that this signifies "the death kneel" for both the U.S. and Japanese economies. It portrays to the world, not only a very bigoted approach to this logical and lucrative opportunity, but it "cuts one's nose to spite one's face" and guarantees them a much stronger drift into isolationism, all while their fiscal ships are sinking.

In attempting to know and understand this man Vladimir Putin, most Western authors have openly demonstrated their ineptitude to truly listen. They mistakenly mislead their audiences down a one-sided path which however finitely describes the environments around him, or a series of events wherein, he has taken action. Yet nowhere do they ever afford the reader an opportunity to sit on his side of the table. There's a glaring aspect about this man which remains forever fervent throughout his life and that is, "he is a man of his word". If Vladimir Putin says he's going to do something, he neither dilutes his pledge, nor exaggerates it. He just does it, following through in a smooth execution. So it is in all honesty, from "this author's perspective", that I say, "To truly know Vladimir Putin is to listen".

During this past July of 2015 the BRICS leaders assembled in Ufa, Russia. Therein the BRICS leaders held a "limited attendance meeting" to which President Putin gave this noteworthy speech as follows:

"It is a pleasure to welcome all my colleagues and friends at another BRICS Summit. Today we are going to discuss the entire range of issues dealing with interaction within our association, coordinate and make new important decisions designed to further raise the authority of our organization and its influence on the political and economic processes. Russia attaches great significance to this summit and we try to do everything to make our joint work substantive and fruitful, beneficial for the development of our economies and citizens".

"We continue our meeting in expanded format with the participation of our delegates. In line with the agenda, we will have a detailed discussion of the pressing issues pertaining to BRICS activities, primarily in the economic sphere. The organization's member States play an important role in the global economy. At the end of last year, the BRICS aggregate GDP extended $32 trillion, which is a 60% growth since the foundation of BRICS, accounting for almost 30% of the global GDP. BRICS nations produce a third of the world's industrial products and half of agricultural goods. We have huge human resources: 43% of the world population – this is an enormous consumer market with a constantly growing demand for modern goods and services".

"Close economic cooperation ties the BRICS nations closer together. International trade is growing – it has gone up 70% since 2009 while Russia's trade with its member States for instance, has doubled. Last year the BRICS economies attracted 20.5% of the world's total direct foreign investment, which in 2009 the number stood at 16.9%. The shares of our countries investment on the global markets has gone up significantly – from 9.7% to 14%. Significant work has been done to strengthen economic cooperation between the BRICS nations. I would like to note that we see this as support from all our partners in this organization and I would like to thank you colleagues, for this".

"Significant work has been done to implement the resolutions of last year's summit in Fortaleza, Brazil. One of the top achievements was the launch of the BRICS Contingent Reserve Agreement and the NEW Development Bank. Our countries have successfully completed the ratification of the relevant agreements. We have approved the procedures for the Contingent Reserves Arrangement bodies and appointed heads of the New Development Bank: Mr. Kamath representing India is the bank's President and vice-presidents from Russia, Brazil, China and South Africa will assist him in his work. The Contingent Reserve Agreement with a capital of $100 billion will make it possible to timely and adequately respond to financial market fluctuations. The New Bank in its turn, with a capital of another $100 billion, will implement large-scale development projects in the organization's member States. We expect to see the first ones launched next year. As we have seen earlier today during the meeting with representatives of the BRICS Business Council, companies from our countries are ready to create joint ventures and enhance mutual investment and trade".

"Among the documents prepared for approval by the summit is the BRICS Economic Partnership Strategy through 2020. It sets the task of making our economies more competitive on the global markets, strengthening ties in energy, high-technology, agriculture, science and education. Russia has also drafted a roadmap for BRICS investment cooperation. We expect our partners to contribute to it so we could finalize the document before the end of the year. We had consultations with our business representatives and already placed some 50 projects and business initiations on this roadmap. These include a proposal to set up an Energy Association, create an International Center for Energy Studies and a Foundry Union".

"The joint use of navigation systems, including the Russian GLOSNASS, opens up broad opportunities. Russian companies are interested in developing cooperation in such areas as production of medical and electronic equipment, software and others. We also propose launching within the framework of this organization, a mechanism for joint studies of competition and unification of anti-trust regulation, developing closer cooperation on the subjects of labor and employment, population and workforce migration – as I already said today, I had a detailed discussion on this issue with the leaders of BRICS trade union organizations. They supported Russia's initiative to hold meetings of relevant ministers. Russia considers broader humanitarian cooperation within BRICS of major importance. The Agreement on Cooperation and Culture that our ministers are to sign today aims at further deepening the friendly ties between our peoples".

"The year of Russia's Presidency saw the first meeting of the Civic BRICS, the BRICS Parliamentary and Youth forums. We are working on the issue of creating a BRICS Network University

and we are analyzing the initiative to create a Council of the Regions of the BRICS nation. The launch of a 'virtual secretariat' will contribute to further reinforcement of the organization's institutional foundation. This modern internet portal will make it possible to further simplify interaction between our countries, while the public will get access to current information on the BRICS activities. These and many other products developed during Russia's Presidency have found their reflection in the Ufa Declaration and Action Plan. These are complex documents that we are to approve at the end of our meeting; they set the key targets not only for the coming year, but for a longer term as well".

During this historic Ufa BRICS Summit, President Putin held one final press conference dwelling on the topic of the Shanghai Cooperative Organization (SCO), on July 10th, 2015. During this event President Putin stipulated that one of the priority tasks for the SCO is to improve cooperation in global finance, while noting the creation of a center of project financing was a vital prospect to the project. "Of the priority tasks is improving cooperation in the financial sphere. We are participating in the work for creation of the SCO Development Bank and special account. The idea of establishing an international project financing center on the basis of the SCO inter-bank association seems promising", Putin said.

Other important options for the SCO lay in Moscow's hopes it might become a platform for solving international issues, such as those with India and Pakistan. The president went onto to say, "We hope that the SCO platform will become an extra forum where we will be able to look for compromises and solutions for disputes issues together. We must solve the issue with full-fledged inclusion of India and Pakistan". Earlier in the southwestern Russian city, New Delhi and Islamabad entered into an ascension process of political, economic and security alliance with signed documents.

During the press conference president Putin further stated, "There is a decline in the rate of growth in the United States. It is well-known that the levels of debt are higher than the levels of GDP there. I'm afraid to be mistaken, but I think that the GDP of the century is $17.8 trillion, while the debt is $18.2 trillion. This is a serious issue not only for the United States, but for the entire world economy", said Putin during the press conference.

The highest U.S. State debt in the world and the biggest ever, now plagues the U.S. Since the end of 2007 it has doubled that level. It is enough to make President John F. Kennedy rock and roll in his grave that the U.S. Congress since 1960, has had to act 78 times to increase the debt limit permanently or temporarily, according to the U.S. Treasury Department. At this writing in late 2015, the U.S. government could again possibly run out of money, according to the Congressional Budget Office (CBO).

President Putin said that, "China remains the engine of the world economy, despite its current issues". At present, an economic slowdown is facing China. The average growth of the local Chinese economy in 1979 – 2010 was 9.9%, according to the China National Bureau of Statistics (NBS). For 2014 China's economy was on the slowest pace in 24 years, growing still at a robust 7.4%. Vladimir

Putin stated, "I agree with the Chinese estimates, which consist of the fact that in the previous period...there has been a certain downward correction, but the latest data shows a slight rise again. So there is nothing special here".

A substantial contribution of Chinese companies is being hoped for by Moscow, for development of Siberia and the Far East of Russia. President Putin commented, "I believe that the Chinese companies could make a substantial contribution to those plans' task we concern ourselves with, they could take part in solving them. With profits for themselves, of course".

On the issue of the Iranian Nuclear Program, President Putin said, "All negotiators have their own opinions, including on sanctions. We stand for the full scale lifting as soon as possible, because we do believe that this is not the right way to solve interventional questions and issues. All of the participants of those talks have their own opinions, compromise must be found. I believe it will be found in the near future".

Nowhere in the Zionist-owned U.S. media has it ever been mentioned that Israel's nuclear program runs roughshod over international law, has "never" permitted inspections, has "never" signed the International Non-Proliferation Agreement and yet has not only never been sanctioned, but continues to receive billions of dollars in U.S. aid. If Israel continues to not be held accountable, this "U.S. double-standard of the law" for Muslim countries will become both useless and meaningless. When it comes to Israel, U.S. presidents following Kennedy, have no clothes.

On September 28, 2015, President Vladimir Putin made a very historic speech while addressing the 70th session of the U.N. General Assembly. Here is its unofficial translation:

"Your Excellency Mr. President,

Your Excellency Mr. Secretary-General

Distinguished Heads of State and Government,

Ladies and Gentlemen",

"The seventieth anniversary of the United Nations is a good occasion to both take stock of history and talk about our common futures".

"In 1945, the countries that defeated Nazism joined their efforts to lay solid foundations for the post-war world order. Let me remind you that the key decisions on the principles guiding the cooperation among States, as well as on the establishment of the United Nations were made in our country – in Crimea, in Yalta – at the meeting of the anti-Hitler coalition leaders".

"The Yalta system was actually formed in travail. It was born at the cost of tens of millions of lives and two world wars that swept the planet in the 20th century. Let us be fair – it helped the humanity through turbulent, at times dramatic events of the last seven decades. It saved the world from large scale upheavals".

"The U.N. is unique in its legitimacy, representation and universality. It is true that lately the U.N. has been widely criticized for supposedly not being efficient enough and for the fact that the decision-making on fundamental issues stalls, due to insurmountable differences – first of all among the members of the Security Council. However, I would like to point out that there have always been differences in the U.N. through all these 70 years. The veto right has always been exercised by the United States, the United Kingdom, France, China, the Soviet Union and Russia alike".

"It is absolutely natural for such a diverse and representative organization. When the U.N. was established, its founders did not in the least think that there would always be unanimity. As a matter of fact, the mission of the organization is to seek and reach compromises. Its strength comes from taking different views and opinions into consideration".

"Decisions abated within the U.N. can either be taken as resolution or not. As diplomats say, they neither 'pass, nor don't pass'. Whatever actions a State takes bypassing this procedure are illegitimate, run counter to the U.N. Charter and defy international law".

"We all know that after the end of the Cold War, a single center of domination emerged in the world. And then those at the top of that pyramid were tempted to think that if we are so strong and exceptional then we know better than anyone what to do, why at all should we reckon with the U.N., which instead of automatically authorizing and legitimizing necessary decisions, often creates obstacles, or in other words, 'stands in the way'. It has now become commonplace to say that in its original form the organization has become obsolete and completed its mission".

"Of course the world is changing and the U.N. must remain consistent with its natural form. Russia is ready to work together with all partners on the basis of general consensus, but we consider attempts to undermine the authority and legitimacy of the United Nations, as extremely dangerous. They can lead to the collapse of the entire architecture of international relations. Then indeed we would be left with no other rules than the rule of force. We would get a world dominated by selfishness, rather than collective work. A world increasingly characterized by dictate, rather than equality, genuine democracy and freedom. A world where truly independent States would be replaced by an ever growing number of de-facto protectorates and externally controlled territories".

"What is the State sovereignty after all? It is basically about freedom and the right to choose freely one's own future for every person, nation, or State. In the same vein goes the question on so-called legitimacy of State authority. One should not play with, or manipulate words. Every term in international law and international affairs should be clear, transparent and uniformly understood criteria. We are all different and we should respect that. No one has to conform to a single development model that someone has once and for all recognized as the only right one".

"We should all remember what our past taught us. We also remember certain episodes from the history of the Soviet Union. 'Social experiments' for export attempts to push for changes within other countries, based on ideological preferences often led to tragic consequences and to degradation, rather than progress. It seems however, that far from learning from other's mistakes, everyone just keeps repeating them. And so the export of revolutions this time of so-called 'democratic ones' continues".

"Suffice it to look at the situation in the Middle East and North Africa. Certainly political and social problems in this region have been piling up for a long time. And people there wished for changes. But how did it actually turn out? Rather than bringing about reforms, an aggressive foreign interference has resulted in a flagrant destruction of national institutions and the lifestyle itself. Instead of the triumph of democracy and progress we got violence, poverty and social disaster. And nobody cares a bit about human rights, including the right to life".

"I cannot help asking those who have caused this situation: do you realize now what you have done? But I am afraid no one is going to answer that. Indeed policies based on self-conceit and belief in one's exceptionality and impunity have never been abandoned. It is now obvious that the power vacuum created in some countries of the Middle East and North Africa led to emergence of anarchy areas. These immediately started to be filled with extremists and terrorists".

"Tens of thousands of militants are fighting under banners of the so-called 'Islamic State'. Its ranks include former Iraqi servicemen who were thrown out into the street after the invasion of Iraq in 2003. Many recruits also come from Libya, a country whose statehood was destroyed as a gross violation of the U.N. Security Council Resolution 1973. And now the ranks of radicals are being joined by the members of the so-called 'moderate' Syrian opposition, supported by the Western countries who first armed and trained them and then they defected to the Islamic State".

"Besides, the Islamic State itself did not just come from nowhere. It was all initially forged as a tool against undesirable, secular regimes. Having established a foothold in Iraq and Syria, the Islamic State has begun to actively expand to other regions. It is seeking dominance in the Islamic World and it plans to go further than that".

"The situation is more than dangerous. Under the circumstances it is hypocritical and irresponsible to make loud declarations about the threat of international terrorism, while turning a blind eye to the channels of financing and supporting terrorists, including the proceeds of drug trafficking and illicit trade in oil and arms. It would be equally irresponsible to try and manipulate extremist groups and place them at one's service, in order to achieve one's own political goals, in the hopes of 'dealing with them' or in other words, liquidating them later".

"To those who do so I would like to say: Dear Sirs, no doubt you are dealing with rough and cruel people, but they are in no way primitive. They are just as clever as you are and you never know who is manipulating whom. The recent data on arms transfers to this most 'moderate' opposition is the best proof of it. We believe that any attempts to play games with terrorists, let alone to arm them, are not just short-sighted, but 'fire hazardous'. This may result in the global terrorist threat increasingly engulfing new regions, especially given that Islamic State camps train militants from many countries, including the European countries".

"Unfortunately, Russia is not an exception. We cannot allow these criminals who have already felt the smell of blood, to return back home and continue their evil doings. No one wants this to happen, does he"?

"Russia has always been firm and consistent in opposing terrorism in all its forms. Today we provide military and technical assistance both to Iraq and Syria, which are fighting terrorist groups. We think it is erroneous to refuse to cooperate with the Syrian government and its Armed Forces, who are valiantly fighting terrorism face-to-face. We should finally acknowledge that no one but President Assad's Armed Forces and Kurd militia are truly fighting the Islamic State and other terrorist organizations in Syria".

"Dear Colleagues, I must note that such an honest and direct approach of Russia has been recently used as a pretext to accuse it of growing ambitions, but the recognition of the fact that we can no longer tolerate the current state of affairs in the world. In essence, we suggest that we should be guided by common values and common interests, rather than ambitions. We must join efforts to address the problems that all of us are facing on the basis of international law and create a genuinely broad international coalition against terrorism".

"Similar to the anti-Hitler coalition, it could unite a broad range of forces that are willing to resolutely resist those who just like the Nazis, sow evil and hatred of humankind. And naturally the Muslim countries are to play a key role in the coalition even more so, because the Islamic State does not only pose a direct threat to them, but also desecrates one of the greatest world religions by its bloody crimes. The ideologists of militants make a mockery of Islam and pervert its true humanistic values".

"I would like to address Muslim leaders – your authority and your guidance are of great importance right now. It is essential to prevent people recruited by militant force from making hasty decisions. And these who have already been deceived and who, due to various circumstances, found themselves among terrorists, need help in finding a path to a normal life, laying down arms and putting an end to fratricide".

"As the current President of the Security Council, Russia will shortly convene a ministerial meeting to carry out a comprehensive analysis of threats in the Middle East. First of all we propose to discuss whether it is possible to agree on a resolution aimed at coordinating the actions of all forces that confront the Islamic State and other terrorist organizations. Once again, this coordination should be based on the principles of the U.N. Charter".

"We hope that the international community will be able to develop a comprehensive strategy of political stabilization, as well as social and economic recovery of the Middle East. Then there would be no need for new refugee camps. Today the flow who were forced to leave their homeland has literally engulfed Europe. There are hundreds of thousands of them now and there might be millions before long. In fact, it is a new great and tragic migration of peoples. And it is a harsh lesson for the Europeans".

"I would like to stress, the refugees undoubtedly need our compassion and support. However the only way to solve this problem at a fundamental level, is to restore the statehood where it has been destroyed, to strengthen the government institutions where they still exist, or are being reestablished, to provide comprehensive assistance – military, economic and material – to countries in a difficult situation; and certainly to those people who will not abandon their homes, despite all the ordeals".

"Naturally, any assistance to sovereign States can and must be offered, rather than imposed, but exclusively and solely in accordance with the U.N. Charter. In other words, everything in this field that is being done, or will be done pursuant to the norms of international law, must be supported by our universal organization. Everything that contravenes the U.N. Charter must be rejected. Above all, I believe it is of the utmost importance to help restore government institutions in Libya, support the new government of Iraq and provide comprehensive assistance to the legitimate government of Syria".

"Colleagues, ensuring peace and regional and global stability remains the key objective of the international community, with the U.N. at its helm. We believe this means creating a space of equal and indivisible security which is not for the select few, but for everyone. Yes, it is a challenging, difficult and time-consuming task, but there is simply no other alternative".

"However, the bloc-thinking of the times of the Cold War and the desire to explore new geopolitical areas, is still present among some of our colleagues. It is regrettable however, that some of our colleagues have so far chosen a different path – that of exploring new geopolitical spaces. First they continue their policy of expanding NATO and its military infrastructure. Then they offered the post-Soviet countries a false choice – either to be with the West, or with the East".

"Sooner or later this logic of confrontation was bound to spark off a grave, geopolitical crisis. This is exactly what happened in Ukraine, where the discontent of the population with the current authorities was used, a military coup was orchestrated from outside that triggered a civil war as a result. We are confident that only through full and faithful implementation of the Minsk Agreements of February 12, 2015, can we put an end to the bloodshed and find a way out of the deadlock".

"Ukraine's territorial integrity cannot be ensured by threats and force of arms. What is needed is a genuine consideration for the interests and rights of the people in the Donbass region and the respect for their choice. There is a need to coordinate with them, as provided for in the Minsk Agreements, the key elements of the country's political. These steps will guarantee that Ukraine will development as a civilized State, as an essential link in building a common space of security and economic cooperation, both in Europe and in Eurasia".

"Ladies and Gentlemen, I have mentioned a common space of economic cooperation on purpose. Not long ago it seemed that in the economic sphere, with its objective market laws, we would learn to live without dividing lines. We would build on transparent and jointly formulated rules, including the WTO principles stipulating the freedom of trade and investment and open competition. Nevertheless, today unilateral sanctions circumventing the U.N. Charter have become almost commonplace. In addition to pursuing political objectives, these sanctions serve as a means of eliminating competition".

"I would like to point out another sign of growing 'economic selfishness'. Some countries have chosen to create closed and 'exclusive' economic associations with their establishment being negotiated behind the scenes, in secret from those countries' own citizens, the general public and business community. Other States, whose interests may be affected are not informed by anything either. It seems that we are about to be faced with an accomplished fact that the rules of the game have been changed, in favor of a narrow group of the privileged, with the WTO having no say. This could unbalance the global economic space".

"These issues affect the interests of all States and influence the future of the world economy as a whole. That is why we propose discussing them within the U.N., WTO and G20". Contrary to the policy of 'exclusiveness', Russia proposes harmonizing regional, economic projects. I refer to the so-called 'integration of integrations', based on universal and transparent rules of international trade. As an example, I would like to cite our plans to interconnect the Eurasian Economic Union and China's Silk Road Economic Belt. We still believe in harmonizing the integration processes, within the Eurasian Economic Union and the European Union is highly promising".

"Ladies and Gentlemen, the issues which affect the future of all people including the challenges of global climate change. It is in our interests to make the U.N. Climate Change Conference to be held in December in Paris, is a success. As part of our national contribution, we plan to reduce by 2030, the greenhouse gas emission to 70-75% of the 1990 level".

"I suggest however, we should take a wider view on this issue. Yes, we might defuse the problem for a while by setting quotas on harmful emissions, or by taking other measures that are nothing but tactical. But we will not solve it that way. We need a completely different approach. We have to focus on introducing fundamental new technologies inspired by nature which would not damage the environment, but would be in harmony with it. Also, they would restore the balance between the biosphere and techno-sphere, upset by human activities. It is indeed a challenge of planetary scope, but

I am confident that humankind has an intellectual potential to address it".

"We need to join our efforts. I refer first of all, to the States that have a solid research base and that have significant advances in fundamental science. We propose convening a special forum under the U.N. auspices for a comprehensive consideration of the issues related to the depletion of natural resources, destruction of habitat and climate change. Russia would be ready to cosponsor such a forum".

"Ladies and Gentlemen, it was in London on January 10th, 1946, that the U.N. General Assembly gathered for its first session. Zuleta Angel, a Columbia diplomat and the Chairman of the Preparatory Commission opened the session by giving I believe, a concise definition of the basic principles that the U.N. should follow in its activities which are free will, defiance of scheming and trickery and spirit of cooperation".

"Today his words sound as a guidance for all of us. Russia believes in the huge potential of the United Nations, which should help us avoid a new global confrontation and engage in strategic cooperation. Together with other countries, we will consistently work towards strengthening the central, coordinating role of the U.N."

"I am confident that by working together we will make the world a peaceful and safe place, as well as provide conditions for the development of all States and nations. Thank You"!

Chapter II

Death of the Western Man

Perhaps the most driving element behind Vladimir Putin's increasing appeal by Western men is the crisis in American masculinity itself. Many Western males either greatly admire, or envy this man Putin. His culture which he avidly cultivates and upholds, naturally grants all men the freedom "to be a man". There's no better evidence to this fact than in the shining "role model" Mr. Putin naturally projects, without any apologies required and free from any overly sensitive, myopic Western political correctness.

America's burgeoning incidents of indiscriminant, public mass shootings is "a male psychosis". This is evident to the fact that they are being denied role models and feasible routes to success. This has permeated into American society by the very same entities who

are behind "global destabilization". They've destabilized Palestine, Iraq, Yemen, Afghanistan, Libya, the Ukraine and almost Syria (where much credit goes to Mr. Putin for putting a stop to it).

However, many forget or are generationally unaware that ever since 1964 they've been ever slowly, silently and even subliminally destabilizing American society itself. They've destabilized colors and then its cultures and now their infecting the sexes. The Zionist stranglehold of America's Wall Street, advertising agencies, major media networks, Hollywood and discrimination policy-shapers, all serve as the major core trace elements to this destabilization virus itself.

In my opening chapter of my prior book, "Tandem 'Escape to the multipolar world", I make reference to a British general and historian, Sir John Bagot Glubb (1887 – 1897), better known as "Glubb Pasha". In his 1978 book, "The Fate of Empires and the Search for Survival" Glubb found that various empires had undergone the same cultural changes in a sequential order of phases or steps. He narrowed these down to 7 major phases which are as follows:

1) Age of outburst and initial "pioneering phase".

2) Age of "conquests".

3) Age of "commerce" (BRICS current phase).

4) Age of "affluence".

5) Age of "intellect".

6) Age of "decadence" (U.S. current phase).

7) Age of "decline".

Western authors, experts and sociologists have all attempted in coming to grips with the terms of the plight of the Western man. While some prefer to interpret this dilemma as purely a sociological development, others conclude it to be a demographic matter where males from childhood to adulthood experience emotional upheaval, confusing roles and identity crisis.

To accurately assess just what exactly is pushing "Mature Western Man" into becoming "an endangered species", let us first eliminate the irrelevant ones most popular today. Of these, 3 come to mind:

1) Identity Crisis
2) Declining male attainment in education
3) Higher divorce rates, meaning men without fathers

It can be said that the causes for number one, share a domino effect with the following two. In the case of identity, the duration of the U.S. as "empire" has thus far prevailed in appearance for some 240 years (1776 – 2016). But as I stand by my conclusion in

"Tandem's" Chapter 3: "The Day America Died; Empires in Decline", America died on the inside, be it by silent coup or otherwise, precisely 53 years ago. Hence this degradation of the "Western Male" has been slowly conducted all the while for the past 53 years. So as an empire who's authentically existed for only 187 years, it's been operating the past 53 years as purely a facade, with something very different within itself.

This profound duality that's taking place is the very root of many of America's ills, including its male identity crisis. For a society to pride itself on the principles, ideals and moral fiber of an era-gone-by is to "live a lie". To live a lie is psychotic, a degenerative strain of schizophrenia whose prerequisite demands self-denial. To live in self-denial is neurotic as it sentences the spirit's sense-of-self to a myriad wasteland of inner damnation, wandering in a continuous meandering of being lost, holding the spirit hostage while preventing any truthful manifestation of self.

The amount of damage this unleashed beast (U.S.-Israel, Bilderburg-Bankers, and Industrial Military Complex) has done in just 53 years is enormous. It has nicked its own people on the home front, eroded small businesses worldwide, while causing death to millions in convoluted, orchestrated wars. President Vladimir Putin is wise to scrutinize big Western businesses, as they have a proven track record of destroying small businesses, while crushing a cultural, compassionate and civic minded sense of community, beneath the wheel.

Slowly over time, as America was silently overtaken after the Kennedy assassination and transcending from its "age of affluence" to its "age of intellect" the robber barons who took control, completely retooled and tinkered with the "Western Man's Identity". Suddenly he no longer stood for truth and justice, but conformity, blind obedience and ass-kissing. For "women's rights" to have arrived on the scene only made their mischievous deeds all the more easier. They pragmatically through media and legislation, replaced oversight with a blind eye, good with evil, masculinity with a neutered boy, compassion and ethics with greed being good and one could write a list a page long.

To remain fair and open minded, I will share others' professional interpretations here shortly, as it pertains to the dilemma of the Western Man. From my own standpoint the reasons are very simple and easy to diagnose. America has been under siege for more than half a century. The fact that it has agreed to cooperate with it means that it has made a deal with the devil. For Americans to suddenly awaken from their slumbers and proclaim that they don't want to play this game anymore, would create extremely polarized friction within its atmosphere. You see, the devil never tears up his contracts.

To back up what I have just stated, in 2002 Israeli Prime Minister Benjamin Netanyahu stated, "Once we squeeze all we can out of the United States, it can dry up and blow away". Not ten years following that statement the U.S. Congress invited this man to speak to them. He received 29 standing ovations during his speech, 4 more than the United States' own president received for his State of the Union Address of the same year. This tells you who America's governing body actually fears and it also tells us who is actually ruling the United States currently.

Not even Winston Churchill, during the 1939 – 1941 period when he and his countryman desperately needed America's assistance against Hitler, was he ever invited to speak to Congress and even if he had he would not have done so without the complete approval of the U.S. president. The U.S. Congressional conduct is one in the same as it is with Kim Jong-un of North Korea. And this is precisely where the United States is headed like a runaway train, to an existence as a North Korean type superpower for Israel where, much like the U.S. Congress demonstrated, its citizens will eventually be subjugated to a lifetime of bowing until it hurts just to receive enough food to sustain themselves!

Marriage being an integral part of Western society, is today passé. When the new overlords of its society support music industries who promote an image that it's cool to do drugs, have random sex with males living like gangster dogs who've half a dozen kids living around town from three different mothers, there's little mystery to its ills. They have been purposely farming the fatherless murders of tomorrow as just another piece to their destabilization project.

Marriage serves adulthood. The marriage rate in America today is well under half the 1969 levels. In the West, less people are getting married, while waiting longer to say "I do". In 1940 only 8% of all households then, consisted of people living alone. Today it constitutes a whopping 30%. Less than a decade ago, 66% of Americans lived as married households. Today that figure is approaching 50%. What good single men remain in America today, have a very low percentage of friends (sometimes just 1, 2, or none) and they feel under-loved, unappreciated, not respected fully and are unfulfilled.

Earlier we made note of "Declining male attainment in education". Thirty-five percent of women ages 25 – 35, have college degrees. For Western males its 25%. And while the women's percentages are increasing, the males' is descending. Christina Hoff

Sommers mentions in her book, "The War Against Boys: How Misguided Feminism is Harming our Young Men", that it is now a fact in America that "Women are significantly more literate and more educated than their male counterparts and this is likely to create a lot of social problems". Not having a sufficient amount of well-educated men will breed an ever larger amount of sophisticated ladies in waiting atop an ivory tower, for a prince that shall never come. Hence, a society of single old maids and girlish, frustrated old boys.

America is quickly becoming a fatherless nation. The vitality and influence of fathers within their families has declined to critical proportions. There has been a progressive loss and dilution of his power in and over his family. Professor David Popenoe, a sociology professor at Rutgers University states, "If present trends continue, the percentage of American children living apart from their biological fathers will reach 50% by the next century. This massive erosion of fatherhood contributes mightily to the major social problems of our time.... Fatherless children have a risk factor of two or three times that of fathered children, for a wide range of negative outcomes, including dropping out of high school, giving birth as a teenager and becoming a juvenile delinquent".

According to David Blankenhorn, author of "Fatherless America", Chairman of the National Fatherhood Initiative and founder/president of the Institute for American Values, combined with research conducted by Rutgers Professor Popenoe and other researchers, for the studies of U.S. society:

- Approximately 30% of all American children are born into single-parent homes and for black communities, that figure is 68%.

- Fatherless children are at a dramatically greater risk of drug and alcohol abuses, mental illness, suicide, poor educational performance, teen pregnancy and criminality, according to the U.S.

Department of Health and Human Services, National Center for Health Statistics.

- Over half of all children living with a single mother are living in poverty, a rate 5 to 6 times that of kids living with both parents.

- Child abuse is significantly more likely to occur in single parent homes, than in intact families.

- 63% of youth suicides are from fatherless homes, according to the U.S. Bureau of the Census.

- 72% of adolescent murderers grew up without fathers.

- 60% of America's rapists grew up the same way, according to a study by D. Cornell (et al), in "Behavior Sciences and the Law".

- 63% of 1,500 CEO's and human resource directors said it was not reasonable for a father to take a leave after the birth of a child.

- 71% of all high school dropouts in America come from fatherless homes, according to the National Principals' Association Report on the "State of High Schools".

- 80% of rapists motivated with displaced anger, come from fatherless homes, according to a report in "Criminal Justice and Behavior".

- In single-mother families in the U.S. 66% of young children live in poverty.

- 90% of all homeless and runaway children are from fatherless homes.

- Children from low-income, two parent families outperform students from high-income, single-parent homes. Almost twice as many high achievers come from two-parent homes than one-parent ones, according to a study by the Charles F. Kettering Foundation.

- 85% of all children exhibiting behavioral disorders come from fatherless homes, according to a study by the Center for Disease Control.

- Of all violent crimes against women committed by intimates, about 65% were committed by either boyfriends, or ex-husbands, compared with only 9% by husbands.

- Girls living with non-natal fathers (boy-friends and step-fathers) are at a higher risk for sexual abuse than girls living with natal fathers.

- Daughters of single mothers are 53% more likely to marry as teenagers, 111% more likely to have children as teenagers, 164% more likely to have a premarital birth and 92% more likely to dissolve their own marriages.

- A large survey conducted in the late 1980's found that about 20% of divorced fathers had not seen their children in the past year. Fewer than 50% saw their children more than a few times a year.

- Juvenile crime, the majority of which is committed by males, has increased six-fold in the United States since 1992.

- In a longitudinal study of 1,197 fourth-grade students, researchers observed, "greater levels of aggression" from mothers-only households than in boys from mother-father households, according to a study published in the Journal of Abnormal Child Psychology.

- The Scholastic Aptitude Test scores have declined in the U.S. more than 70 points in the past two decades. Children in single-parent families tend to score lower on standardized tests and to receive lower grades in school, according to a Congressional Research Service Report.

- America has paid a dear price for making that deal with the devil. This country America is not just faced with a loss of fathers, but the virtue of fatherhood as well. By society blatantly discounting the necessity of the position, it has only amplified the dilemma. Noted family historian from Princeton University, Lawrence Tone commented, "The scale of marital breakdowns in the West since 1960 has no historical precedent that I know of. There has been nothing like it for the last 2,000 years and probably longer".

During the "baby bust" of the 1970-1984 period in America, only 50% of the children born then, still lived with their natural parents by age 17. That was an abrupt drop from the 80% previously. So we can see that the time period I had pointed to, as being the "Death of America" (1963) is ever more likely to be accurate. America's lifestyles and standard of living then were on the upswing. Family values mattered, wealth-sharing with corporations was a reality and such as it was, "Truth, Justice and the American Way" prevailed.

Why is it then that the only places you find this happening today, are in nations like "Russia"? When the Israelis' destabilization, Bilderberg's Federal Reserve and the CIA's Industrial Military Complex took down a U.S. president, things changed forever in America. And they changed due to a complete lack of "push-back". Docile Americans did nothing, they accepted it, they surrendered and they made a deal with the devil which is beginning to show.

An overthrown America was told, "William Greer didn't kill the president, it was a Russian" and Americans fluttered their sheepish eye lashes and said, "O.k., we can believe that". And they were told the USS Liberty Incident "was an accident", that in the Gulf of Tonkin Incident "they shot at us first" and that the 9-11 Incident "had no Israeli involvement" and that the slew of wars which followed "happened this way" and not "the actual way". And Americans again fluttered their sheepish eye lashes again and again and again and again, with no push-back and replied, "O.k., we can believe that". Unfortunately, when you roll over and play dead long enough only to live lies, you have sentenced yourself to a perpetual existence as that of "a walking dead". And judging from the tell-tale signs of research and statistics, America has become just that.

In researching father-family involvement one notices a dangerously lopsided amount of research is fixed only on the mothers and children. Organizations and healthcare agencies often omit fathers. Beginning with pregnancy, labor and delivery, practically all appointments are made for mothers that is often during times when father's work. This goes for pediatric visits as well. Family services and school records in the United States today, usually carry the child's and the mother's name in labelling, but not the father's. Inside most family agency buildings the décor is typically pastel with photos of mothers, babies, dogs and flowers, while the waiting room reading material is for women and most of the staff greeting you there are women.

In the case of most U.S. welfare offices, most case planning meetings do not invite fathers. When their home visitor is greeted at the door by a man, most often they will ask to speak with the mother. Under these conditions, American fathers quickly get the message of being irrelevant for their children's well-being, except when it comes to financial support. Rutgers' Professor Popenoe and his colleagues reviewed the role of fathers raising children. They found significant variations in comparison for that of mothers. An overlooked element of fathering for instance, is "play". From child birth through adolescence, fathers seem to favor play over caretaking.

Researchers have discovered that play is far more vital to development than previously realized. It can be physically stimulating, while exciting the senses. Play can be instrumental for learning about relationships, teamwork, competition and being in-sync with ones abilities. A father's way of playing can affect everything from emotions to intelligence, as well as academics. A father's play is also a noteworthy contribution of promoting the essential virtue of self-control.

A committee of the Board of Children and Families of the National Council, had this to say about fathers, "Children learn critical lessons about how to recognize and deal with highly charged emotions, in the content of playing with their fathers. Fathers in effect, give children practice in regulating their own emotions and in recognizing other's emotional clues". Whether at play or other situations, fathers tend to emphasize competition, challenges, taking initiative and risk-taking, as well as independence. Mothers as caretakers gravitate towards instilling emotional security and personal safety. The involvement of fathers appears to be connected to the improvement of quantitative and verbal skills, problem-solving and higher academic achievement for children. Men are also vital in the promotion and concept of cooperation and the soft virtues.

Married family life and child rearing can encourage men to understand prudence, cooperation, honesty, trust and self-sacrifice. It is a civilizing force for men, with the power of instilling such positive, behavioral changes as, setting a good example.

In the British journal of Social Psychology, Mark Finn and Karen Henwood wrote, concerning the issue of masculinity and fatherhood. In it they argue that the traditional view of masculinity, with its focus on power, aggression, economic security and "maleness", when compared with the new Western views of fatherhood, which incorporate many aspects of motherhood, is a source of struggle for many men who become fathers.

Timothy Allen Pehlke and his colleagues conducted a study of fatherhood in popular (Zionist) T.V. sitcoms. In them they concluded that fathers were generally shown to be relatively immature, unhelpful and incapable of even caring for themselves, in comparison to other family members. The researchers also stated that they found fathers to often serve as the butt of the family member's jokes. Though these characterizations were done with humorous intentions, it nonetheless depicted fathers as being socially incompetent and objects of derision. This would serve as an obvious example of U.S. networks' "intentional destabilization" by their Zionist producers and networks, in affiliation with the degenerative agenda imposed by the new powerbrokers (part of that contract with the devil).

Researcher Suzanne Flannery Quinn conducted a study of the depiction of fathers in best-selling children's picture books. Of the 200 books studied, only 35 had shown the mother and father being together. Quinn concludes, "Because fathers are not present, or prominent in a large number of these books, readers are given only a narrow set of images and ideas from which they can construct an understanding of the cultural expectations of fatherhood. It appears the decline of fatherhood issue and male identity crisis could be interrelated".

Ray Williams, in one of his Psychology Today articles titled, "Our Male Identity Crisis, What Will Happen to Men?", Williams says, "In a post-modern world lacking clear-cut borders and distinctions, it has been difficult to know what it means to be a man and even harder to feel good about being one. The many boundaries of a gendered world built around the opposition of work and family-production, versus reproduction, versus cooperation and hard vs soft have all been blurred, leaving men groping in the dark for their identity".

The male identity and men's portrayal in current Western societies seems mostly negative. The image today is almost akin to what had happened to women being demonized and marginalized in a heavily biased tint. The Western male's identity crisis issue is of vital importance since males much more than women, are now being treated for ADHD, making-up the majority pool of poor students, are committing more suicides and crimes and are dying younger. To a lesser extent, researchers also attribute the rise of artificial insemination use, as well as recent successful experiments in growing artificial male sperm in laboratories.

Within the rise of Western divorce rates, child custody is most often granted to mothers. The continual Zionist media's portrayal of casting men in a negative light, together with the feminization of men and the absence of fatherhood in society, creates confusion and frustration in younger generation males. It is noteworthy to consider the studies of various societies, in terms of gay men and homosexuality. Genetically speaking, less than 0.05% fit into this category. Yet there has been a groundswell campaign by destabilizing forces within the Western establishment, to "promote" this as a preference of lifestyle choice. Hence, Western Man now also must contend with his society's open and accepted undercurrents which make attempts to lure and herd him into a gay lifestyle, hoping to catch him off guard in the midst of his blurred identity's lost role. Western males often do not currently have any definitive role models anymore and in turn, are at a greater loss for defining their role in society.

Once traditionally having been received as successful breadwinners, patriarchs of families and respectable leaders and heroes, Western men recently have been reduced to be the butt jokes within its pop culture media. Nathanson and Young a Canadian research group, did an in-depth study of the changing roles of men through media. They found that T.V. programming like "The Simpsons" portrayed Homer the father character, as being lazy, chauvinistic, irresponsible and ignorant, with a son Bart who was constantly mischievous, rude and cruel to his sister. This was presented against a backdrop of a kind, thoughtful and considerate mother and daughter. It is as if the network barons were telling Western Man to "stay stupid and wear it proudly". The vast majority of advertisements and T.V. programming in the study found men to be presented as ignorant buffoons, aggressive evil tyrants, or insensitive, shallow studs for women's pleasure.

In J.R. MacNamara's book, "Media and the Male Identity: the Making and Remaking of Men", positive reflections of men in the media was found in less than 20% of all instances studied. In the review the "overlords of destabilization" shows up again, as 55% of all media reporting of male activities involved violent crimes, murder, assault and armed robberies. MacNamara concluded that over 30% of all media discussion concerning male sexuality, was in relation to pedophilia. To throw gasoline on a raging fire, Western media moguls frequently project males in T.V. movies as lacking in commitment when in relationships and often cheating on women.

Guy Garcia, author of "The Decline of Men: How the American Male is Tuning Out, Giving up and Flipping Off His Future" says, "Women really have become the dominant gender. What concerns me is that guys are rapidly falling behind. Women are becoming better educated than men, earning more than men and generally speaking, not needing men at all. Meanwhile, as a group men are losing their way". Men are felt to be splintering their identity in instances where husbands are being expected to accept non-traditional family roles such as childcare, housework and cooking, while wives bring home the bacon in bigger paychecks. Rutgers' Professor Popenoe contends, "The crisis of fatherhood then, is ultimately a cultural crisis, a sharp decline in the traditional sense of communal responsibility. It therefore follows that to rescue the endangered institution of fatherhood we must regain our sense of community".

Once crowds of women went to work in factories during World War II, made famous by "Rosie the Riveter". While their men fought abroad they assumed this role as a temporary, yet necessary position. Once the "real men" returned, it was an unspoken assumption that the women could then resume being "real women". There currently appears to be a new assumption in America today, that men are now women. In March 2010 the Wall Street Journal published a two page story titled, "Why Women Don't Want Macho Men". It contended that women of prosperous Western societies favored men with more feminine features. It made further claims that women of developing countries still favored masculine men. What some critics of the article questioned were, "Does this really mean that Western women want to be the traditional man"?

When put to the question, most American women still insist that they prefer physically fit and handsome, masculine-looking men who are self-reliant, handy and can provide a reasonable sense of protection. Keeping in mind that the publication in question is heavily Zionist-controlled and in exploring the article further it seems to reflect bias by associating societies where women prefer "girlie-men" as being healthier, yet it produces no evidence to back-up its claims. Some of the strongest societies in modern times can be seen in places like Russia, which still has no hesitation to embrace masculinity. A surprising statistic has proven that matriarch societies have always failed and died. Famous ancient queens might have inspired but they produced no leadership. The "face that could launch a 1,000 ships" didn't lead anybody. It lured warriors with enticing dreams. What the propaganda of the Wall Street Journal fails to mention is that the largest percentage of women it surveyed for their study were from European countries, soon to lose their sovereignty, where the sacrament of marriage was already in intensive care and their regions were better known as "single-mother nations". The weighted majority of professionals who have studied both the male issues vs history all agree on the following: "A girlie-man nation is on a fast track to hell; the death of a society".

To discuss the role of men in America today, if one were to toss the topic out onto any social table, they would be met with an embarrassing silence. What's the American male's role today; what are they in charge of? Sadly, the only supposed and accepted norm seems to be "to cede their unfair advantages over to the female gender". As the West's male species here watches the grains of sand to his fate quickly fleeting in time, he seems to howl a silent cry for help, over a herd of masses who either aren't listening, or have yet attained an ability to listen. It is a peculiar affair being male in America today and its role has been hijacked and sent off course in a perplexing direction to ruin. What's my advice? "Move to a developing nation". There will surely come a time when America will miss you dearly, but why mope around feeling sorry for yourself when there's millions of young ladies waiting offshore who'd not only be proud to have you, but who can still naturally give you the freedom every day, "to just be a real man".

Chapter III

Virtue and Nature's Insurmountable Odds

Vladimir Putin's religion finds its roots in the concepts of Orthodox Christian Civilization. Its basis believes that Jesus Christ's presence becomes satisfied within men seeking to build a kingdom of God on Earth. This interpretation is taken from a scripture of the Orthodox tradition known as the "Symphony of Church and State". In it the Church is portrayed as being the soul of the State, while the State is suggested to be the body. In what Russian Orthodox members assume to be a harmonious partnership, they sense the Church as preparing them for heaven, with the State maintaining their culture in a transformation of Church influence.

It is also important that at the new level, the relations between Church and State are developing. They are true partners with joining their efforts in resolving relevant, internal and global tasks. They are implementing joint endeavors for the benefit of their homeland and its people. For many years Russia has become stronger.

Vladimir Putin is perceived by his nation's majority, as not only the Head of State (the nation's body), but also as a Russian Orthodox Church's prominent member (the soul). Perhaps for one to best comprehend where this nation and its relationship with its faith gets such persistent, unbreakable bond in its culture and tradition, try to conceive that it is "500% older than the United States".

These days the Russian Orthodox Church and the whole Orthodox world are commemorating the one thousand and twenty-fifth anniversary of the Baptism of Russia. The Christianization of Russia predetermined the destiny and civilizational choice of Russia. Orthodoxy has become a Spiritual pillar. It's bound by close ties of kinship, Russia, Ukraine and Belarus.

What further galvanized this culture's rare longevity in survival were the most atrocious forms of torture and genocide ever committed in the recorded history of humankind, performed against these people during the Bolshevik Revolution. Some "66 million" of them, over a thirty year period were tortured, raped and slowly murdered by the Jews. It is estimated it would take 11 holocaust museums just to fill one Russian Megacaust.

It is no small wonder then that with America now being under the control of the Orthodox people's former tormentors, that Putin finds himself today rebuking the West for its deviant, sexual mores and sick spirituality. Today many nations are revising their moral values and ethical norms, eroding ethnic traditions and difference between peoples and cultures. Society is required not only to recognize everyone's rights to freedoms of consciousness, political views and privacy, but also to accept without question, the equality of good and evil. The Middle East has witnessed many persecutions against

Christians, in which President Putin has asked the world's political leaders for their help in putting a stop to it. The Russian President spoke to a meeting with Orthodox Christian leaders in Moscow

stating his alarm, "In many of the world's regions, especially in the Middle East and in North Africa, inter-confessional tensions are mounting and the rights of religious minorities are infringed, including Christians and Orthodox Christians. This pressing problem should be a subject of close attention for the entire international community. It is especially important today to make efforts to prevent intercultural and interreligious conflicts, which are fraught with the most serious upheavals".

The Orthodox Churches and the Russian State's growth of cooperation was praised by Putin as he stated, "We act as genuine partners and colleagues to solve the most pressing domestic and international tasks, to implement joint initiatives for the benefit of our country and people".

The Russian Federation, while being condemned by many European leaders, passed legislation making it illegal to promote homosexuality. Putin added that the Church was giving Russians a moral compass at a time when many were seeking help. He said,

"Today when people are once again searching for moral support, many of our compatriots see it in religion. They trust the wise, pastoral word of the Russian Orthodox Church". Over the past 1,000 years the church was ultimately responsible for the rise and development of "culture and education" in Russia. Putin added, "The adoption of Christianity became a turning point in the fate of our fatherland, it made it an inseparable part of the Christian civilization and helped it turn into one of the largest world powers".

Patriarch Kirill, head of the Russian Orthodox Church warned at the same meeting, that a "civilization catastrophe" would occur if Christians were pushed out of Syria. In addressing the crisis facing Christians in the Middle East, Kirill and other Orthodox leaders were critical of the U.S. and other Western leaders for their lack of response. To commemorate the 1,025[th] anniversary of the "Baptism of Russia", the leaders of all 15 Orthodox Churches were present to honor this official adoption of Christianity and the establishment of the Russian Orthodox Church of Kievan Rus by Prince Vladimir in 988 A.D.

The growing secularist suppression of Christian freedoms, where "gay marriage" has been created, such as non-Muslim countries like Britain, was condemned by Orthodox leaders at the meeting. The Chief Ecumenical Officer of the Russian Orthodox Church, Metropitian Hilarion said, "Secularization in disguise of democratization is leading Western nations toward totalitarianism. Powerful energy today strives to finally break with Christianity, which controlled its totalitarian impulses during 17 centuries. Eventually it unconsciously strives to set up an absolute dictatorship that demands total control over each member of society. Don't we move to it when 'for the sake of security' we agree to obligatory electronic passports, computerized fingerprint identification for everyone and photo cameras appearing everywhere"?

Metropitian Hilarion went onto to expose France's creation of "same sex marriage" as an attempt to make "immorality normal", accusing the French government of "consciously and demonstratively ignoring the demands of the peoples, using teargas to disperse them". President Putin, Patriarch Kirill, along with then Ukrainian leader Viktor Yanukovyck, took part in a prayer session at a reception in Kiev.

Directly addressing the Slavic peoples, Patriarch Kirill spoke of genuine unity, adding that it is the Orthodox religion that creates it. He stated, "Our ancestors adopted the Christian faith and together with it, a system of values and morals that no historical upheavals were able to destroy." There exists a strong, shared, spiritual foundation which unites Russians, Ukrainians and Belarusians, more than their own national boundaries can divide them. In a most direct posture Patriarch Kirill, in addressing the same-sex marriage fad sweeping the Western world he warned, "This is a very dangerous, apocalyptic symptom and we must do everything so that sin is never validated by the laws of the State, in the lands of the Holy Rus because this would mean that the people are starting on the path of self-destruction".

In shifting his focus from the perils of spiritual damnation to the plight of the earth's ecosystems, Vladimir Putin familiarized himself with the works of a research expedition from the Severtsov Institute of Ecology and Evolution, while on a trip to the Alexandra Land Island, on the Franz Josef Land Archipelago. While he became more informed about the institute's studies of polar bears, he visited the Russian border guard's northern most checkpoint. The Ministry of Civil Defense, Emergencies and Disaster Relief, as well as the FSB Border Guard Service, issued Mr. Putin their final report on the joint exercises being carried out there. With the Nagurskoyo Artic border checkpoint airfield being their destination, Vladimir Putin was accompanied by Deputy Prime Minister Sergei Sheigu and the Head of FSB Border Guard Service and Presidential Envoy in the Northwestern Federal District, Ilya Klabanov.

In a Taiga off-road vehicle, Mr. Putin was taken to the expedition's base camp of biologists from the Institute of Ecology and Evolution. The use of GPS transmitters to study polar bears were first used in Russia by this Institute's biologists' team. Shortly after his arrival, Vladimir Putin joined Dr. Vyacheslav Rozhnov, the Deputy Director of the institute and Head of the expedition, in one of the tents. Dr. Rozhnov made mention that the Russian Geographical Society received a million rubles grant towards this program, designed to preserve and restore the polar bears' population. Information concerning the habitat, migration and population of polar bears, is gathered and collected by the institute's research biologists.

Negative factors that might affect the bears' habitat, such as pollution of the Artic, are being evaluated. Practical recommendations for creating conditions to support the polar bears' survival and increase population growth is the production of this work. The Russian section of the Artic is home to 6,000 of the globe's 25,000 polar bears.

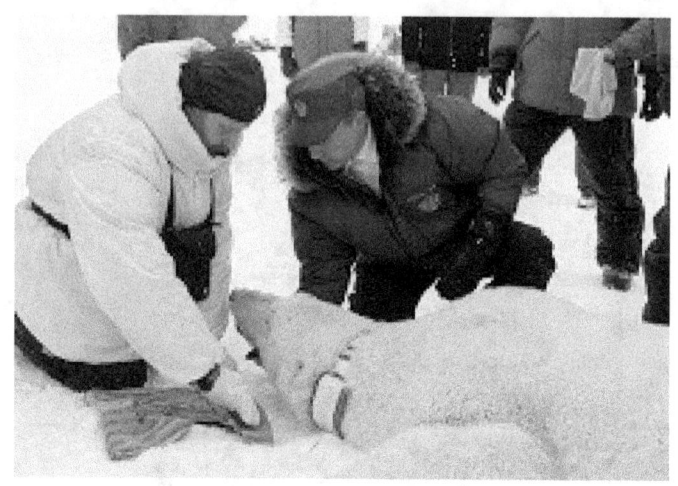

Seeming in his natural element, Putin and the biologists used a customized trap to catch a polar bear, which weighed 231 kg. They also measured the animal before administering a GPS collar, which greatly aids both the study and monitoring of these magnificent creatures. Following a brief photo session with the expedition members, Vladimir Putin then went onto gain first-hand knowledge of one of the Arctic's prominent issues, while visiting Severnaya Bay.

"Environmental pollution" was assessed as the leading problem affecting the bears' habitat, at that moment in time. In a 1995 – 2005 polar geological survey expedition, it was estimated that 250,000 barrels containing 40,000 – 60,000 tons of oil products, over one million scrapped metal drums, lubricants, oil in barrels, coal and hardware including aircraft, radars, trucks and buildings, had all been abandoned on the archipelago. A total of 100 hectares was strewn with refuse in the Severnaya Bay, where ships for civil and military supplies were brought.

Vladimir Putin, perhaps in disgust after having looked at the rows of barrels frozen into the ground, said that the Arctic needs to be cleaned up. He has since ordered a widespread clean-up of Russia's Arctic regions. "Geopolitically, Russia's deepest interests are linked to the Arctic", said Putin. "Here Russia's security and defense capabilities is provided for. Here there are vitally important transport communications". Some 90 billion barrels of oil and one-third of the world's undiscovered natural gas, lie beneath the Arctic region. In August of 2007, Canada's Foreign Minister was scathing after Russian explorers inside a mini-submarine, plunged to the bottom of the Arctic Ocean and planted a rust-proof, Russian metal flag. Under U.N. rules, if Moscow can prove this then it is entitled to economic rights over a far larger slice of the Arctic region; beyond the usual 350 – mile limit from its coast.

One of the world's rarest predators, the Amur (Ussuri) tiger lives in Russia's Far East and is registered in the International Red Data Book. Once numbering some 100,000 a century ago, today the Ussuri tiger population has evaporated to just 4,000. Roughly 450 of these species live in Russia's Primorye (Maritime) Territory and the Amur Region. Vladimir Putin was joined by Chief Veterinarian Doctor of the Moscow Zoo, Mikhail Shentsky in August of 2008.

With the aid of a traquilizer gun (and Putin's astute marksmanship), they managed to immobilize a five year old female. Russian Academy of Sciences' Scientists, of the Severtsov Institute of Ecology and Evolution presented a transmitter neck straps to Putin, for monitoring the health of tigers, as well as their migratory routes of travel.

Senior Researcher, Viktor Lukaretsky or the Russian Academy of Sciences Institute of Ecology and Evolution, along with Vladimir Putin, conducted an examination of the five year old tigress. Mr. Putin administered a GPS-Argos transmitter neck strap on the female tiger. He has also been credited on some such research adventures, to have been instrumental in safe-guarding the welfare and safety of camera crews. Russian scientists are the first in this sphere to implement these independent projects to study the Ussuri tiger.

Though photographers often attempt to accentuate an aura of machoism around Vladimir Putin, his natural abilities are in no need of exaggeration. He fishes in Russia's Altai region, can commandeer both Russia fighter jets, as well as bombers, maneuver a Formula 1 race car, hang-glide with migratory birds, ride and handle horses, scale cliffs, arm wrestle, teach and perform Judo, tranquilize tigers and bears, ride motorcycles and high-speed snowmobiles, deliver James Bond caliber moves on the ski slopes and dive into icy cold streams to swim. It is no hidden wonder why Vladimir Putin is a "genuine man", nor why he has such a popular following, even among Western men and women.

Though I possess neither the time nor the money to copyright the following terms, on this December 5th, 2015 I hereby proclaim to be their founder and that is "The Belt of Eden" and/or "Eden's Belt". Upon various studies of data and forecasts from many different physicists and scientists, I have concluded that there will come a time when "Climate Change" can no longer be slowed

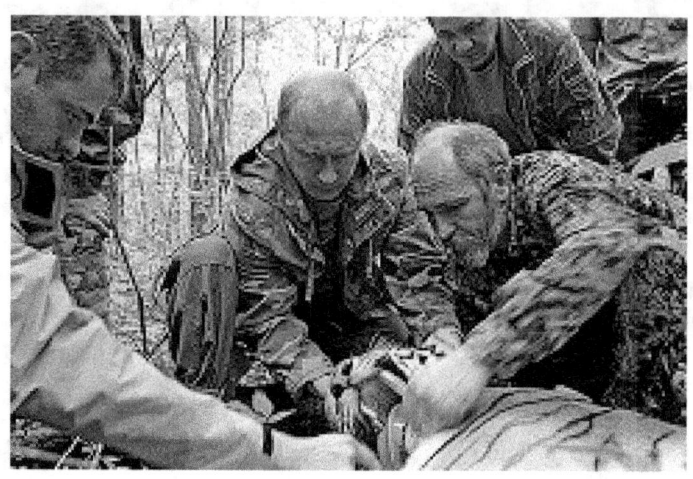

down. Much to my dismay, I am baffled at the large percentages of people who either remain dumbfounded to the phenomena, or actually believe that they can "reverse" this process. It is "not" reversible, I assure you. The environment has been overly toyed with, to an extent to which a "regeneration stage" has been set into motion. Once this train leaves the station there's no calling it back.

What I term to be described as "Eden's Belt", or the "Belt of Eden" I've concluded to be the last remaining strip around the planet, which will support human life, once the regeneration phase reaches its climax. Located between the 50 degree and 60 degree North latitude parallels, it's no small wonder why America's greedy elitists would like to get their hands on Russia, as it is strategically situated within the catbird's seat of survivability and sustainability. The U.S. (along with most of China) won't even have a prayer.

This conceptual interpretation suggests the possibility that an "Armageddon" may not necessarily involve nuclear weapons, but rather a worldwide, mad-max outburst on the day "there's no more room at the inn". Much like a lifeboat, once the point in time has been reached, where taking in one more survivor means the death to all onboard, Russia will lock the doors. However, being the

authentic realist that I am, I always reserve both the right and open-mindedness to be wrong.

During 2013 at a conference on Cooperation and Development in the Arctic, President Putin announced, "Keeping a balance between extraction of resources and conservation of fragile ecosystems is a key priority of Russia". The conference opened in

Arkhangelsk, as Vladimir Putin went onto to say, "With almost a third of the country belonging to the Far North, Russia has a special responsibility for the Arctic. One of our priorities is to keep the balance between the economic activity and the preservation of the unique environment and respect for the culture and traditional way of life of the indigenous peoples". This was recited by Secretary of Russia's Safety Council, Nikolay Patrushev in a greeting, TASS reported.

Vladimir Putin remarked, "Russia favored the strengthening of cooperation with the member countries of the Arctic Council on all directions". He mentioned that the climate and ecology of the whole planet were being directly influenced by the natural processes in the region. He was confident that within the conference would emerge practical recommendations for the efficient settlement of tasks facing the international community in the Arctic.

What will go down in history as a milestone in 21st century imperialism, the actions of a portion of Western States that were performed shortly following this speech made by Vladimir Putin were beyond criminal. One might even say they nearly beg to invite Armageddon. I'm referring to the Israeli colony the U.S., along with Israel itself, Turkey and Saudi Arabia creating ISIS and then, along with the U.K. and even Germany, never approached Russia, the U.N. Security Council, Assad, or even his "democratic government" before engaging in active war within the country of Syria. How would this be received then, if say for instance Russia and China just got up one day and decided to say, "Oh my, we've noticed some terrorists over there in Los Angeles" and proceeded to drop 6,000 sorties on the State of California without asking? Am I getting through to you here? "Where's the exceptionalism"? Oh I see, you mean "exceptionally criminal, exceptionally corrupt and exceptionally reckless and wrong". I get it.

In exactly 70 years from the date most of these nations (France, Germany, U.K., U.S.) signed the Anti-Hitler Coalition in Yalta, Russia the obsession in Nazi-like expansionism has suddenly blanketed an ever-maddening Western ideology, in a pandemic fever of international law-breaking, complete circumvention to debate and respect for authority and a blatant disregard for democratic principles. But let's not kid ourselves any longer shall we? Just as the West has used ISIS as a tool, so is Israel using the West as one. One that they dream will deliver them their ultimate, demented fantasy of world domination and control. No disrespect to my Jewish acquaintances, "but didn't the Jews learn anything from the Nazi experience"?

In Putin's own words, "It seems however, that far from learning from other's mistakes, everyone just keeps repeating them". It was President Putin himself, who at the September 28, 2015 U.N. General Assembly's 70th year, reminded every one of its founding principles; "Free will, defiance of scheming and trickery and spirit of cooperation".

Nearly 75% of Western civilization's citizenry is now ingesting some form of anti-depressant. Could this be attributed to the fact that their governments are not only running roughshod over the U.N. Charter, all free nations' sovereignty, and now them as well? While all their media continually feeds them lies, which they are aware are lies, it herds the masses towards anti-depressants, the modern societies' last step before revolution. Hitler himself was quoted, "If you tell a big enough lie and tell it frequently enough, it will be believed"!

The West's Liberal Totalitarian States are becoming belligerent, dangerously reckless, exceedingly desperate, genocidal and completely unconvincing. Going berserk in extremes of false-flagging 14 victims in the San Bernardino shootings and another 130 innocent victims in their 2015 Paris charade, was made a pathetic and toxic pretext for the U.S. - Israeli colony, France, Germany and the U.K. to escalate their military involvement inside Syria. But the reasons presented to a tenderized public had little to do with being guilty of supporting State-sponsored terrorism. Hence, the West's war on terrorism has come to a complete failure, because it is terrorism.

Need I remind you, that this has now all come down to "the slime leading the slime"? We're dealing with entities within our Western governments who invent "terrorism" and manufacture "terrorists" to help them move illegal shipments of oil, arms and narcotics, while serving as a taxpayer-funded excuse to increase their funding, as well as to keep pinching back at the taxpayers' rights in their own countries. This in turn, completely reduces all of Western civilization into now being nothing more than fish-in-a-barrel. "Medicated" fish, I might add!

In 1915 1,198 lives were lost in the sinking of the Lusitania, yet the United States refrained from entering into World War I. But the United States is gone now. This is made clearly evident by the shear disposition to its current, very "un-American" conduct. Nowhere in the United States first 187 years of its history, can you find where it acted strangely, peculiar, convulsive and imperialistic in military escalations which gleamed of desperation. Where's the oversight, the investigative reporting, debate and cooperation?

In the context of the Syrian civil war there is clear indication of Western foreign policy being naive and grossly inconsistent. Having been correct all along, the undeniable truth in Russian foreign policy is yet ignored by Western governments. Being utterly racist and discriminatory with Zionist hate, this "new phase of terror" has been well evaluated by Yuri Glushchenko, leading researcher of the Russian Institute of Strategic Research, Candidate of Economic Sciences. In his objective analysis shared by him and other experts, the United States today insists to associate "anything" related to Islam as "terrorists". Yet when a dozen black people are indiscriminately gunned down in a prayer meeting by a white member, it is classified as "a hate crime", which then commutes the offense to fall under a different set of criminal statutes. Muslims currently comprise some 1.7 billion members worldwide, or roughly 20% of the planet's population. A number too great it seems, for Godless, Zionist Jews to handle.

The playbook never changes with these people. Hate-ridden, frustrated and unfulfilled Zionists create and make terror, blame it on the Muslim world and then use America as their tool to go jousting with windmills. Meanwhile, Angela Merkel's sanctions against Russia (another Zionist windmill they can add to their list) has proceeded to bring %300 – 500% more damage and harm to her own citizens than it ever has affected Russia.

There is too much product and not enough demand in the world. One dandy of a global recession is crashing to earth and the West is frantically making panic decisions in the great shadow of its $220 trillion counterfeit, quantitative easing schemes. As it has been said by many, "when all else fails, they take us to war". Trade wars, then currency wars, then real war. This archaic routine has already played out so many times in history; "can't somebody out there please come up with a more civilized solution"?

Though the idea of war in the Middle East is rejected by the majority of Western States' citizens, with the clock ticking down to the final bursting of their sinful, fiscal bubbles in air, Zionist insiders take on a frenzied rush to whip up great fear in their media networks. How ironic it is that the nation with the deepest reservoirs of truth still remaining, during all these events, is none other than "Russia".

Russia's Minister of Defense in December of 2015, presented compelling evidence of a highly lucrative, stolen oil operation, between Turkey and ISIS, under the watchful eyes of the United States. This evidence was shown in graphic, video detail with sophisticated clarity. Truck convoys in Eastern Syria loaded stolen Iraqi and Syrian oil by ISIS, while the U.S. as policeman, goes on the take and looks the other way. In one day, 1,772 oil trucks were counted (..., may I remind you that Turkey is a member of NATO).

The U.S. State Department came to Turkey's defense and denied the claim, which bared Americans even further reasons to continue consuming those mass quantities of antidepressants.

Now, let me get this straight? A U.S. president can be impeached for sponsoring a burglary (Nixon-Watergate), but if he gives the green light for his military to help smuggle heroin, steal oil from a sovereign State, all while sponsoring, training and arming terrorists, that's o.k.? "...., pass me one of those pills, would you....,".

Chapter IV

A Message to Russians

Having the deepest of respects for Russian President Vladimir Putin, though I feel I can contribute some valuable lessons along to the Russian people and everyone else reading this, I feel that its only common courtesy to first hear what their great president has to say. I will resume my contributions following this historic, great speech.

The following is President Putin's December 3rd, 2015 Annual Presidential Address to the Federal Assembly. Members present for this occasion were of the Federation Council, State Duma deputies, members of the government, heads of the Constitutional and Supreme Courts, regional governors, heads of regional legislative assemblies, heads of Russia's traditional religious faiths, public figures, including heads of regional civic chambers and the heads of Russia's biggest media outlets.

President of Russia, Vladimir Putin:

"Citizens of Russia, members of the Federation Council, State Duma deputies, I would like to begin my address with words of gratitude to the Russian servicemen who are fighting international terrorism".

"Today here in the St. George Hall, a historic hall of Russian military glory, we have combat pilots and representatives of the Armed Forces who are taking part in the anti-terrorist operations in Syria. Gelena Peshkova and Irina Pozynich, who lost their husbands in the war against terror, have joined us too. My deepest respect to you and the parents of our heroes".

"I would like us to all honor the memory of the soldiers who gave their lives while doing their duty, and the memory of all Russian citizens who fell at the hand of terrorists". (Moment of silence)

"Colleagues,

Russia has long been at the forefront of the fight against terrorism. This is a fight for freedom, truth and justice for the lives of people and the future of the entire civilization. We know what aggression of terrorism is. Russia faced it back in the middle of the 1990's, when our country, our civil population suffered from cruel attacks. We will never forget the hostage crisis in Budennovsk, Beslan and Moscow, the merciless explosions in residential buildings, the Nevsky Express Train derailment, the blasts in the Moscow metro and Domodedovo Airport".

"These tragedies took thousands of lives. We still grieve for them and will always grieve, all with the victims' loved ones. It took us nearly a decade to fully break the backbone of those militants. We almost succeeded in expelling terrorists from Russia, but are still fighting the remaining terrorists underground. This evil is still out there. Two years ago, two attacks were committed in Volgograd. A civilian Russian plane was recently blown up over Sinai".

"International terrorism will never be defeated by just one country, especially in a situation when the borders are practically open and the world is going through another resettlement of peoples, while terrorists are getting regular financial support. Terrorism is a growing threat today. The Afghanistan problem has never been resolved. The situation there is alarming and gives us no optimism, while some of the yet recently stable and well-doing countries in the Middle East and North Africa – Iraq, Libya and Syria – now plunge into chaos and anarchy that pose a threat to the whole world".

"We all know why that happened. We know who decided to oust the unwanted regimes and brutally impose their own rules. Where has this led them? They stirred up trouble, destroyed the countries' Statehood, set people against each other and the "washed their hands" as we say in Russia, thus opening the way to radical activists, extremists and terrorists. The militants in Syria pose a particular high threat for Russia. Many of them are citizens of

Russia and the CIS countries. They get money and weapons and build up their strength. If they get sufficiently strong to win there, they will return to their home countries to sow fear and hatred, to blow up, kill and torture people. We must fight and eliminate them there, away from home".

"That is why it has been decided to launch a military operation there, based on an official request from the legitimate Syrian authorities. Our military personnel are fighting in Syria for Russia, for the security of Russian citizens. The Russian Army and Navy have convincingly demonstrated their combat readiness and their increased capabilities. Modern Russian weapons have proven to be effective, an invaluable practice of using them in combat conditions is being analyzed and will be used to further improve our weapons and our military equipment. We are grateful to our engineers, workers and all other personnel of our defense companies".

"Russia has demonstrated immense responsibility and leadership in the fight against terrorism. Russia people have supported these resolute actions. The firm stance taken by our people stems from a thorough understanding of the absolute danger of terrorism, from patriotism, high moral qualities and their firm belief that we must defend our national interests, history, traditions and values".

"The international community should have learned from past lessons. The historic parallels in this case are undeniable. Unwillingness to join forces against Nazism in the 20th century cost us millions of lives in the bloodiest world war in human history. Today we have come again, face to face with a destructive and barbarous ideology and we must not allow these modern day dark forces to achieve their goals. We must stop our debates and forget our difference to build a common anti-terrorist front that will act in line with international law and under the U.N. aegis".

"Every civilized country must contribute to the fight against terrorism, reaffirming their solidarity, not in word, but in deed. This means that the terrorists must not be given refuge anywhere. There must be no double standards. No contracts with terrorist organizations. No attempts to use them for self-seeking goals. No criminal business with the terrorists".

"We know who are stuffing their pockets in Turkey and letting terrorists prosper from the sale of oil they stole from Syria. The terrorists are using these receipts to recruit mercenaries, buy weapons and plan in human terrorist attacks against Russian citizens and against people in France, Lebanon, Mali and other States. We remember that the militants who operated in the North Caucasus in the 1900's and 2,000's found refuge and received moral and material assistance in Turkey. We still find them there. Meanwhile, the Turkish people are kind, hardworking and talented. We have many good and reliable friends in Turkey. Allow me to emphasize that they should know that we do not equate them with the certain part of the current ruling establishment that is directly responsible for the deaths of our servicemen in Syria".

"We will never forget their collusion with terrorists. We have always deemed betrayal the worst and most shameful thing to do and that will never change. I would like them to remember this – those in Turkey who shot down our pilots in the back, those hypocrites who tried to justify their actions and cover up for the terrorists. I don't even understand why they did it. Any issues they might have had, any problems, any disagreements, even those we knew nothing about, could have been settled in a different way. Plus we were ready to cooperate with Turkey on all the most sensitive issues it had; we were willing to go further, where its allies refuse to go. Allah only knows, I suppose, why they did it. And probably, Allah has decided to punish the ruling elite in Turkey by taking their mind and reason".

"But if they expected a nervous or hysterical reaction from us, if they wanted to see us become a danger to ourselves, as much as to the world, they won't get it. They won't get any response meant for show, or even for immediate political gain. They won't get it. Our actions will always be guided primarily by responsibility – to ourselves, to our country, to our people. We are not going to rattle the sabre. But if someone thinks they can commit a heinous war crime, kill our people and get away with it, suffering nothing but a ban on tomato imports, or a few restrictions in construction or other industries, they're delusional. We'll remind them of what they did, more than once. They'll regret it. We know what to do".

"We have mobilized our Armed Forces, security services and law enforcement agencies to repel the terrorist threat. Everyone must be aware of their responsibility, including the authorities, political parties, civil society organizations and the media. Russia's strength lies in the free development of all its peoples, its diversity, the harmony of cultures, languages and traditions, mutual respect for all dialogues between faiths, including Christians, Muslims, Judaists and Buddhists. We must firmly resist any manifestation of extremism and xenophobia while defending our ethnic and religious accord, which is the historical foundation of our society and the Russian statehood".

"In 2016 we will hold elections to the State Duma. I would like to remind party leaders, all participants of the upcoming election campaigns and all social and political forces about the following words of our famous historian, Nokolai Karamzin: 'Those who have no respect for themselves cannot hope to be respected by others'. That does not mean that love for our homeland must blind us into saying that we are better than all others in everything we do. But Russians must know their value. Yes we can debate ways to solve this or that issue, but we must remain united and remember what is most important for us: 'Russia'. The election campaign must be honest and transparent and respect the law and the electorate. At the same time, it must be conducted so as to win public trust in the election result and legitimacy".

"Colleagues, I expect that a considerable part of the parliamentary candidates' election programs will be devoted to the issue of corruption, which is a major concern for society. Corruption is hindering Russia's development. Officials, judges, law enforcement officers and deputies at all levels, are obliged to submit their income and expense declarations and declare their property and assets, including outside Russia. From now on, State and municipal officials will have to disclose information about the contracts they plan to sign with the companies of their relatives and friends. Situations with a possible conflict of interests will be closely monitored by the regulatory and law enforcement authorities, as well as civil society".

"Just recently, participants in the Russian Popular Front's project For Fair Public Procurement, told me about instances of abuse and blatant violations they have uncovered. I asked the Prosecutor General's Office and the law enforcement authorities to promptly react to this information. The law must be hard on those who are guilty of premeditated crimes against human lives and the interests of society and the State. But the law must be lenient to those who have slipped up. Today, nearly half of the criminal cases brought to court concern petty crimes or misdemeanors, but those who committed them, including the very young people, go to prison for them. A prison term and even a prison record usually have highly negative impact on these people's lives, often creating a situation in which they commit new crimes".

"I ask the State Duma to approve the Supreme Court's proposal that some offenses in the Criminal Code are decriminalized and that misdemeanor is classified as administrative offense, with an important reservation: a repeated offense must be classified as a criminal act. We must also work to enhance the independence and objectivity of our courts. In light of this, I suggest strengthening the role of juries and expanding the list of crimes that can be submitted to them. It's not always easy to find 12 jurors and although I know the position of human rights organizations, which insist on 12-member jurors, forming such juries is not easy and it is expensive. Therefore, I suggest cutting the number of jury members from 12 to 5-7, on the condition that they take their decisions autonomously and independently".

"Colleagues, last year we faced some serious economic challenges. Oil and other products we traditionally offer to export fell in price. The access in Russian financial institutions and companies to global financial markets was restricted. I know that many people are experiencing hardships today. These economic issues are affecting incomes and the generally quality of life. I understand very well what these people are wondering, when we are going to overcome these hardships and what needs to be done in order to accomplish this. The current situation is complicated, but as I have said before, not critical. In fact, we can already see some positive trends. Industrial production and the national currency are generally steady. There is a slight decline in inflation. We can see significantly lower capital flight as compared with 2015".

"However, this doesn't mean that we just calm down and wait for everything to miraculously change, or that we can just sit quietly in anticipation of rising oil prices. Essentially, such an approach would be unacceptable. We must be prepared for lower commodity prices and external restrictions to last much longer. By changing nothing we simply run out of reserves and economic growth rates will linger around zero. This is not the only issue to consider. Busy with the immediate tasks, we must not overlook general global development trends. The globally economy is rapidly changing shape. New trade associations are forming. We are experiencing a period of radical change in the sphere of technology. This is a critical moment when countries need to compete to secure their roles in the global divisions of labor for decades ahead. We can and must become one of the leaders".

"Russia has no right to be vulnerable. We must have a strong economy, excel in technology and advance our professional skills. We must make full use of our current advantages, as there are no guarantees that we will have tomorrow. Clearly the authorities must hear the public out and explain the nature of the problems people face and the reasons behind the government's actions, treating civil society and business as equal partners. What areas should we focus on? First, competitive manufacturing is still concentrated most in the commodities and mining sector. We'll only be able to achieve our ambitious goals in security and social development, to create modern jobs and improve the living standards of millions of our people if we change the structure of our economy".

"Importantly, we do have effective industrial and agricultural operations, as well as small and medium sized businesses. Our goal is to have the number of these kinds of companies grow fast in all sectors. Our programs for import substitution and export support, manufacturing, retrofitting and professional training should be geared to achieving this goal".

"Second, we need to bear in mind that a number of industries are now at risk, including the construction, automotive and light industries, as well as railway engineering. To address this, the government will need to come up with special support programs. Financial resources for this purpose has been set aside".

"Third, it is imperative to support low-income households and socially vulnerable groups of citizens and finally adopt fair principles of providing social assistance that is made available to those who really need it. In particular, it is necessary to take into account the industrial needs for people with disabilities and focus on their training and employment. We have done a lot to improve demography, education and healthcare. The key bench marks in these areas were outlined in the corresponding executive orders of May, 2012. Of course life is ever changing and given the current complications, our responsibility for people's welfare only increases, so I'd like to ask you to take these executive orders seriously. We must strive to fulfill them".

"Fourth, it is imperative to achieve a balanced budget. This of course is not an end in itself, but a critical prerequisite for macroeconomic stability and our financial independence. As you may recall, by the end of the 2016 federal budget year the deficit should not exceed 3%, even if revenue is lower than expected. Please take a note of this colleagues, members of the State Duma and the Federation Council, the Federal Assembly in general. This is important. I just mentioned that financial stability and the independence are interrelated. Please keep these basic considerations in mind".

"Budget planning in fact, planning each budget cycle must begin with a clear identification of priorities. We must make government programs play the decisive role in this process again. It is essential that we tighten our control over public funds, including federal and regional subsidies to industrial and agricultural enterprises. I believe that they should be transferred to the user only, through treasury accounts. Government revenue must be used strictly as planned. 'Grey' schemes used in paying customs duties, excise taxes on alcohol, tobacco and fuels and lubricants, siphon off hundreds of billions of rubles from the budget annually. This is outright theft".

"I propose forming a single system for administering tax, customs and other fiscal payments. There are a variety of options to go about this and we discussed them on many occasions. I expect the government to submit specific proposals. Here again, I would like to emphasize that the tax environment for business remain unchanged in the coming years".

"Fifth, we need to further strengthen trust between the government and business, to improve the business climate in Russia. This year we have mostly completed the plans outlined in the national entrepreneurial initiative. The dynamics are good, but we certainly shouldn't stop yet. The government, together with the Agency for Strategic Initiatives and leading business associations, should continue their systematic work to improve conditions for doing business, constantly monitoring how laws are carried out locally. I believe free enterprise to be the most important aspect of economic and social well-being. Entrepreneurial freedom is something we need to expand to respond to all attempts to impose restrictions on us".

"That is why we have given such a broad authority to the newly created Federal Corporation for the Development of Small and Medium Businesses. I would like to ask all ministries, departments, governors, heads of all Russian regions, State-owned companies and banks to provide all the necessary assistance to it".

"Polls show that businesses see no quantitative progress in the regulator's work, yet all the necessary instructions for this have been issued, even more than once. We repeat ourselves and our attempts to reduce their powers. We reduce them in one area – they simply grow again in another. A whole army of inspectors continues to hinder the operation of good businesses. I am not saying that control is not necessary. Businesses require regulation, but I ask the Government Commission for Administrative Reform to work out, together with business associations, proposals on eliminating redundant and overlapping functions of regulatory agencies and submit them by July 1, 2016".

"I would like to cite some figures supplied by one of our business associations. During 2014, the investigative authorities opened nearly 200,000 cases on so-called 'economic crimes'. But only 46,000 of 200,000 cases were actually taken to court and 15,000 cases were thrown out during the hearings. Simple math suggests that only 15% of all cases end with a conviction".

"At the same time, the vast majority, over 80%, or specifically, 83% of entrepreneurs who faced criminal charges, fully or partially lost their businesses – they got harassed, intimidated, robbed and then released. This certainly isn't what we need in terms of a business climate. This is actually the opposite, the direct destruction of the business climate. I ask the investigative authorities and the prosecutor's office to pay special attention to this".

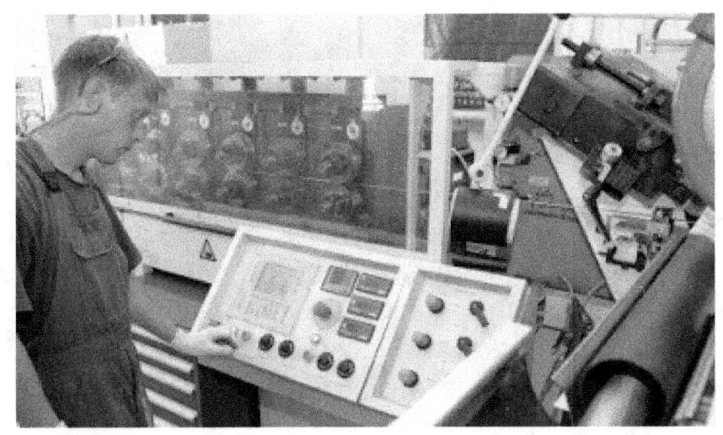

"I would like to emphasize that prosecutors should make greater use of the tools available to check the quality of investigations. I know that discussions have been going on for a long time. About the prosecutors' office's needs. As you know, we have separated the investigative authorities and the prosecutor's office, in order to ensure independent investigations are carried out; it was a conscious decision. Today I remind you, the prosecutor's office has the authority to cancel a decision to institute criminal proceedings, or waive the indictment, or even refuse to support a case in court. We must learn to use what is available to analyze what is happening in practice".

"In addition, I believe that suspects in economic cases should be detained, only as a last resort measure; for the most part, investigators should opt for release on bail, travel restrictions or house arrest. The role of law enforcement and the judicial system is to protect the economy and the community from fraud and criminals and to protect the rights, property and dignity of all those who obey the law and conduct their businesses honestly".

"There is one more point I'd like to make. Last year we announced the so-called amnesty to return financial assets to Russia. Yet businesses seem in no hurry to take advantage of that opportunity, which suggests that the procedure proposed is too complicated, while the guarantees it supplies are still insufficient. I follow the public discussions on the issue. The word is that what we have already done and the decisions made previously are slightly better than the solutions we've offered in years past, but it is definitely not enough today. I ask the government to organize consultations with the business community, with the Supreme Court, with law enforcement agencies and in short order, make the appropriate adjustments. I also suggest extending the capital amnesty itself, for another six months".

"Colleagues, the State will fund the necessary assistance to those who are ready to go forward and become leaders. We are building such a system in our dialogue with the business community based on its requirements and the tasks facing our country. The Industry Development Fund is already supporting import substitution projects. This is included in mechanisms such as the special investment contracts. Some governors directly request this to allow investors to cover their capital outlays on developing new product lines. Obviously we are aware of the regional governors' concerns. The regions should be motivated to consolidate their economic base, so an increase in region profits from implementing these products should not lead to reduction in federal subsidies".

"We are ready to guarantee the demand for the goods produced under these programs and projects. I propose giving the government the right to purchase, on a non-compliant basis, up to 30% of the products manufactured under special investment contracts. Whatever remains should go to the free markets, including those abroad, to motivate these companies to monitor the quality of their products and reduce overheads. As you know, when other countries carried out these programs, the terms for the State support were even tougher, it was mandatory for a certain percentage of goods produced, to be sold abroad. What for? To motivate producers to manufacture quality products".

"We're saying we will guarantee demand in our own market. Our terms are somewhat different from those in other countries with tougher terms. That said, we must assume that these products will be highly competitive on the international market. Let me emphasize again, that we will support expressly competitive domestic product lines. No one should be working under the illusion that under the guise of import substitution it's possible to build a substandard, out of date product and pawn it off to the State, or to our people and make them pay a premium price for it. Russia needs companies that are capable, not only of providing the country with quality products, but also of taking on foreign markets. The Russia Export Center was established to help those that are ready for this effort".

"In addition, I suggest making the growth of non-energy exports one of the key indicators of the performance of industry-related agencies and the government as a whole. I think it would be appropriate to implement the business community's initiative and create a technological development agency to help companies acquire domestic and foreign patents and licenses for engineering services. Access to foreign markets and the expansion of Russian manufacturing should become a natural strategy for the development of the nation's business sector and the entire Russian economy. We should put stereotypes aside and believe in our own capabilities. If we work with this attitude, we are certain to see a result".

"Our agriculture sector is a positive example. Just a decade ago we imported almost half of our own food products and critically depended on imports, whereas now Russia has joined the exporters' club. Last year Russia's agricultural exports totaled almost $20

billion. This is a quarter more than our proceeds from arms sales, or about one third of our profits from gas exports. Our agriculture has made this leap in a short, but productive period. Many thanks to our rural residents".

"I believe we should set a national goal – fully provide the internal market with domestically produced foods by 2020. We are capable of feeding ourselves from our own land and importantly, we have the water resources. Russia can become one of the world's largest suppliers of healthy, ecologically clean, quality foods that some Western companies have stopped producing long ago, all the more since global demand for such products continues to grow".

"To fulfill these ambitious goals we need to concentrate our resources on primary support for highly efficient farms. This approach should underlie the program for the development of the agro-industrial complex. This includes large, medium and small companies – all of them must be efficient. I would like the Agriculture Ministry to pay special attention to this. It is necessary to put to use millions of hectares of arable land that is now idle. They belong to large land owners, many of who show little interest in farming. How many years have we been talking about this? Yet things are not moving forward. I suggest withdrawing misused agricultural land from questionable owners and selling it at auction for those who can and want to cultivate the land".

RUSSIAN MARKET
€10 000 000 000
Annual volume of online transactions
2% of total retail trade

"I would like to ask the government to prepare specific proposals, including drafts regulations and standards by June 1, 2016. I would also like to ask the State Duma deputies and all members of the Federal Assembly to make amendments to the related laws over the next year and adopt laws to make this possible at the next autumn session. We also need our own technology for the production, storage and processing of agricultural produce, our own seed and pedigree stock. This is a very important goal. We are still vulnerable in these areas. I ask you to get leading research centers, The Russian Academy of Sciences and businesses that are successful in putting advanced technology into practice, involved in this process".

"In my previous address, I announced the launch of the National Technology Initiative, spanning 20 years, but practical work is already underway. It shows that we have plenty of storage teams capable of offering and following through on innovative ideas. In areas such as neutron technology, robotics in aviation and the transport sector in general, energy storage and distribution systems, Russia has every chance of breaking through to global markets in the near future, within the next few years. Development institutions should be geared towards achieving priority goals, primarily those related to technological modernization. We have over two dozen of them. Unfortunately many of them to put it bluntly, have turned into dumping grounds for bad debts. It is essential to streamline them and optimize the structure and mechanisms of this work. I know that the government and the Central Bank are actively working on this".

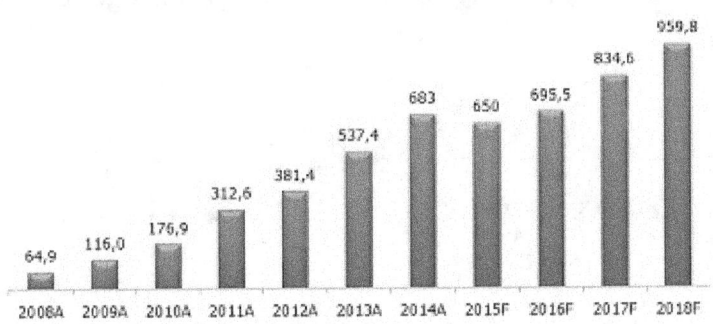

Figure 1. Russian online shopping market volume in 2008-2018, bln RUB

"We should make a more active use of the investment potential of domestic savings for economic modernization. I ask the Central Bank and the government to submit proposal on the development of the corporate bond market, something we have discussed many times. It is essential to simplify the procedure for the issue and acquisition of corporate bonds. To make it worthwhile to investors, individuals to invest in the development of the domestic real sector. I propose exempting the coupon income on these bonds from taxation, including from income tax for individuals".

"Dozens of major projects are being implemented, or are about to be launched in industry, agriculture, transport and housing construction. They should have a positive impact, not only on certain sectors, but also stimulate the comprehensive development of entire territories. These are primarily private projects".

"To expedite their effective implementation it is important to make pinpoint amendments to laws, lift administrative barriers and assist the development of the infrastructure and the process of entering foreign markets. These issues often extend beyond the scope of just one government agency. So I propose putting in place a mechanism to support the most important projects. A special agency can be established for this. I ask Prime Minister Dmitry Medvedev to submit proposals on the work of this agency".

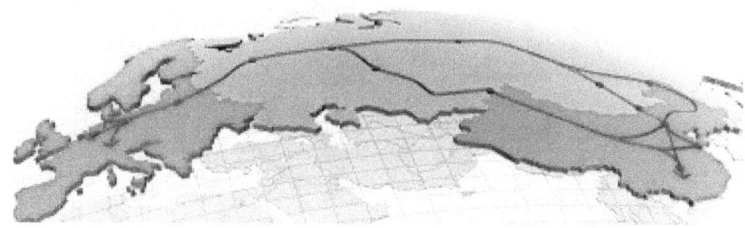

"Incidentally, one such project could be the creation of major, private Russian companies that specialize in online trade, so that Russian goods are delivered via the internet, to all countries in the world. We do have a great deal to deliver".

"Colleagues we are interested in broad business cooperation with our foreign partners, and we welcome investors who focus on long-term work on the Russian market, even though the current circumstances they face aren't always favorable. We highly appreciate their positive attitude to our country and the fact that they see advantages in growing their respective businesses in our country. Russia is involved in integration processes, designed to open additional avenues for expanding economic ties with other countries".

"We have reached the next level of cooperation within the Eurasian Economic Union by creating a common space with free movement of capital, goods and labor. We have reached a basic agreement on combining Eurasian Integration with the Chinese Silk Road Economic Belt. A free trade zone with Vietnam was established. Next year we will host the Russian ASEAN summit in Sochi and I'm sure we will be able to work out a mutually beneficial agenda for cooperation".

"I propose holding consultations, in conjunction with our colleagues from the Eurasian Economic Union, with SCO and ASEAN summit members, as well as with the States that are about to join the SCO, with the view of potentially forming an economic partnership. Together our States make up nearly a third of the global economy, in terms of purchasing power parity. Such a partnership could initially focus on protecting investments, streamlining procedures for the cross-border movement of goods, join development of technical standards for next-generation technology projects and the neutral provisions of access to markets for both services and capital. Of course this partnership should be based on principles of equality and mutual interest".

"For Russia, this partnership opens new possibilities for increasing exports of food and energy, as well as offering service in engineering, education, healthcare and tourism to the Asian Pacific Region, allowing us to play the leading role in forming new technology markets and reorienting major global trade flows to Russia. We will continue to upgrade our transport infrastructure and expand major logistic centers, such as the Azov-Black Sea and the Murmansk transport hubs, modern ports in the Baltic Sea and the Russian Far East. We will consolidate the system of inter-regional air transport, including in the northern and Arctic regions.

We will review in detail the situation with inland waterways and river routes, during the forthcoming State Council meeting".

"The North Route should become a link between Europe and the Asia-Pacific Region. To enhance its competitiveness, we will extend the preferential regime of the free port of Vladivostok to key Far Eastern harbors, as requested by the entrepreneurs who operate in this strategically important Russian region. The socioeconomic development of this region is a major national priority. Investors have shown great, practical interest in the new methods of operation we have proposed, including priority development areas. I instruct the government to expedite decisions on levelling off energy rates and I urge the Parliament to promptly hear the draft law on the free allocation of land plots to people of the Far East".

"Over the past few years, major investments have been made in the development of Khabarovsk and Vladivostok and people there have noticed improvements. Komsomolsk-on Amur must become one more rapidly developing center in the Far East. It is a city with a rich history and modern, high-tech industries, which turn out civilian products that enjoy high demand and also work fruitfully for the defense sector. But this city's urban and social infrastructure has been neglected. I'm referring to the city's face and its sports, culture, healthcare and education facilities, none of which are consistent with the potential of Komsomolsk-on-Amur. This is why it's difficult to attract talented, young professionals there,

which the regional companies badly need. I believe we can use resources under the on-going programs to address the problems of Komsomolsk-on-Amur without delay. Of course we can't do this overnight, but we at least must understand what we need to accomplish and how fast work must proceed".

"Colleagues, we have a long-term agenda that must remain independent of election cycles and the prevailing situation. These strategic goals include preserving the nation, bringing up our children and helping them develop their talents, which constitutes the basis of the power and future of any country, including Russia".

"I'd like to begin with demography. We've registered a natural increase in population for the past three years. It has been modest, but present nevertheless. What I would like to highlight is that according to forecasts, we should have seen a demographic collapse due to the demographic echo of the 1990's, which demographers have predicted, including at the U.N. But this hasn't come to pass, primarily because half of the newborns today are second or third children. Russian families want to have children, they believe in their future and in the country and they are confident that the State will help".

"The maternity capital program ends next year. Over 6.5 million families have enjoyed its benefits, including Crimea and Sevastopol. But we know that our efforts in this sphere have not been sufficient to close the demographic wound of the past. Of course we realize this will be hard on the budget, that the program needs major funding. We said in the past that we need to analyze the figures to see if we can shoulder this burden, as the financiers say, if we can guarantee the payment of these allocations. Yes we can do this despite the current challenges. We believe we must extend the maturity capital program for at least two years".

"A major demographic policy measure is the development of preschool education. Over the past three years, 800,000 new places have been created at kindergartens. Practically in all parts of Russia, such institutions are available for children between the ages of three and seven. I know that the Prime Minister has paid special, personal attention to this. Thank you, Mr. Medvedev. However, so far individual families – many families – continue to encounter problems placing children in kindergartens. As long as these problems exist, we cannot say that the issue has been closed. I ask both the government and regional authorities to pay special attention to this".

"Now, healthcare. The main achievement of our entire policy in this sphere is that we are seeing an increase in average life expectancy. Over the past decade it has increased by more than five years and this year, according to preliminary estimates, should exceed 71 years. Nevertheless there are still quite a few problems that have to be dealt with. Next year the Russian healthcare system will transition completely to an insurance based system. It is the direct responsibility of insurance companies, operating in the compulsory medical insurance system, to uphold patients' rights, including in situations where they are refused free medical care without reason. If an insurance company does not do this, it should be held accountable, including being banned from working in the

140

compulsory medical insurance system. I ask the government to ensure stringent oversight in this regard".

"Next, we have significantly expanded the scope of high-tech medical care. It may be recalled that in 2005, 60,000 high-tech operations were performed in Russia- 60,000! Compared to 715,000 in 2014. For the first time in the country's history, a significant part of such operations are carried out without there having to be a waiting list, and this is indeed a major achievement".

"However, it's important to understand that certain operations are expensive. As a general rule, they are performed at leading federal medical centers and clinics. To finance such operations, I propose establishing within the compulsory medical insurance system....,. We have thought about this a great deal – whether we should provide additional funding to the system. The deputies, government ministers and governors know what happens in reality. The compulsory medical insurance system is a territorial system and it supports primarily territorial healthcare institutions. Naturally, under financing is a matter of concern for the heads of major federal clinics, where the majority of the high-tech operations are in fact performed. So to finance these centers and perform such operations, I propose instituting a special, federal component within the compulsory medical insurance system. I request that the relevant amendments to the law be adopted during the spring session".

"Even though, this is not enough because people must not suffer while we make those decisions. It is necessary to ensure continuous financing of high-tech medical care, including with direct support from the federal budget, until this decision is made. As you also know, the ambulance service has been significantly upgraded as part of the Healthcare National Project. We have procured a large number of modern ambulance vehicles and other equipment. Naturally as time goes on the auto fleet needs maintenance and renovation. Ten years have passed and I remember well, we agreed that we will make an initial injection of federal funding and then the regions will take over the responsibility and keeping the financing at a certain level. But this never happened, which is unfortunate. I understand that there may be issues, but like I said many times before, it is imperative to get our priorities straight. It was the wrong thing to do, to wait for everything to fall apart and expect to be bailed out again with the money from the federal budget. However, the way things are now, it looks like we will have to do it again. But that's not what we agreed upon. In any case, I ask the government and the regional authorities to get back to this issue and resolve it jointly".

"People are complaining that they often cannot understand why certain hospitals, schools, cultural or social centers and institutions are being closed or merged. We keep talking about the need to restructure the network which is in some cases oversized. Yes, that's a fact. But we must proceed very carefully and be fully aware of the fact that in order for us to be able to reach certain indicators, closing rural medical centers is not always the best option. Unfortunately, such things happen. People then have to travel 100 kilometers to get medical attention. This is outrageous! Please make sure that things are done right. I ask the government to draft and adopt a methodology for the most efficient distribution of social institutions by March 1, 2016. It should be mandatory for use in these regions. We must find a legal, valid formula that will allow us to do so".

"In matters such as providing assistance to the elderly, or people with disabilities, or supporting families and children, it is imperative to show more trust in civil societies and non-profit organizations. Often they work more effectively and efficiently, showing genuine concern for the people. Also, there's less red tape in their work. I would like to propose a number of concrete solutions, based on the results of the active citizens' forum community, which took place in November. First, we will launch a special program of presidential grants, to support non-profit organizations working in small towns and villages".

"Second, the non-profit organizations that have established themselves as reliable partners of the State will receive the legal status of a 'non-profit organization – provider of social useful services' and a number of incentives and preferences. Finally, I believe that making up to 10% of the regional and municipal social programs' funding available to non-profit organizations, is the right thing to do. That way, non-profit organizations will be able to participate in providing social services that are financed from the budget. We believe we know well the current legislation and we are not imposing anything on anyone, but I'd like to ask heads of the regions and municipalities to bear this in mind in their work".

"Colleagues, as you may recall there is a meeting with children in Sochi at the Sirius Center for Gifted Children on September 1st. Our children and young adults are really interesting and goal oriented people. We must do our best to make sure that today's students get an excellent education, have opportunities to be creative, choose a profession to their liking and are able to self-actualize, regardless of their geographical location or level of their parent's income. All children must have equal opportunities for a successful start in life".

"Every year schools have more and more students. There will be 3.5 million more of them, over the next decade. It's great, it's good, but it is also very important to make sure that this increase does not afflict the quality of education and learning conditions and that the current level continues to improve. Schools need more space for students. I ask the government to put together, in conjunction with the regions, a specific plan of actions in this regard. A decision was reached to release up to 50 billion rubles from the federal budget next year, to repair, renovate and build new schools".

"I suggest we take a broader look at these issues. Comfort buildings are not enough to get a good education. We need professional and motivated teachers, ground-breaking educational programs and of course, opportunities for the children to engage in creative activities, sports and extracurricular activities. Of course we should use the best of what Palaces of Pioneers and the young technicians' clubs have to offer. We must build our work on an innovative and up-to-date foundation with participation of businesses, higher education institutions and universities".

"I will now note a positive fact, such as the growing interest of young people in engineering jobs and blue-collar occupations, the vocations of the future. Competition for enrollment in engineering universities has almost doubled in the past two years. The World Skills International (WSI) will take place in Kazan in 2019. By the way, Russia was the first to hold such contests for young people, aged 10 to 17 years. It's important to make sure that such tournaments become a road map for school children, for those who are just choosing their trades. We must establish a whole system of national competitions for blue collar workers. I suggest we call this system, 'The Young Professionals'. This is a very important task".

"In a nutshell, Russian schools' additional and professional education and support for children's creative work, should be aligned with the country's future, the requirements of the people, in this case, the young peoples' demands of the economy in the context of its prospects. These guys will have to resolve even more complicated tasks and should be ready to be the best. They should become not only successful in their careers, but also simply decent people with a firm, moral and ethical background".

"Colleagues, we have repeatedly faced an historical choice of which road to take to further development. We crossed another milestone in 2014 when Crimea and Sevastopol were reunified with Russia. Russia declared a voce piena, its status as a strong State with a millennium-long history and great traditions, as a nation consolidated by common values and common goals".

"We are acting with the same confidence now, at a time when Russia is waging an expressly, direct struggle against international terrorism. We are making and implementing decisions knowing that only we can cope with the tasks facing us, but only if we act together. I will cite a quotation that seemed stunning even to me. These words were said by a man who was far removed from politics, Dmitry Mendeleyev who expressed these thoughts more than 100 years ago: 'We will be immediately destroyed if we are divided. Our strength lies in our unity, our warriors, our benign domesticity that multiples the numbers of our people; our strength lies in the natural growth of our intrinsic wealth and love of peace.' These are wonderful words that are pertinent to us today".

"At the same time, Russia is a part of a global world that is changing rapidly. We understand well the complexity and scale of existing problems – both foreign and domestic. There are always difficulties and obstacles on the path to progress and development. We will respond to all challenges, we will be creative and productive, we will work for the common good and for the sake of Russia. We will move forward in unity and working together, we will achieve success. Thank You"!

Since this chapter is devoted to "Russian People", I must first disclose to them from what standpoint I am addressing them from. Though I am a native born American citizen who's a direct descendant of both William Brennan a former, very liberal U.S. Supreme Court Justice and to former U.S. Cavalry guerrilla fighter, General Philip Sheridan, once made famous in the American poem "Sheridan's Ride", as well as to James Donegan, an Irishman who fought in the British Army at the Battle of Waterloo and was later compensated with an estate for saving the life of "The Iron Duke", the Duke of Wellington, I am not an American of today, but rather yesterday.

I make this statement from my innate belief that America died some 50 years ago and what power structure I believe, successfully hijacked it then and to this very day, is not devoted to the true and former principles and ideals of what America used to always stand for and uphold. This truth is blatantly proven, due plainly to the fact that "Russia" now resembles more of "an authentic and genuine moral and ethical democracy, than the current overlords of the modern United States of today"!

As you now well know, Glubb Pasha the former British General and historian I made reference to earlier, narrowed down those "6 primary phases for an empire":

- Pioneering age

- Conquest age

- Commerce age

- Affluence age

- Intellect age

- Decadence and Decline age

Now, right at this moment it is evident that Russia stands at the very same point in time where the U.S. last stood just before it died, during its "Commerce age". You (Russians) now live in the best, most well-positioned country in the world at this very moment in time. So it's no wonder that President Vladimir Putin speaks to address the Federal Assembly, in a manner of great detail and with an all-encompassing sense of extreme importance.

RT News (Russia Today) has a very wise slogan, "Question more"! Had Americans implemented that adage into action in 1963 they would have succeeded in still having a democracy today. So the first lesson in my message to you is to "never accept a coup"! The Americans accepted theirs and in turn they lost everything; their culture, their identity, their traditions, their moral fiber and ethics, along with their ideals, faith and dreams. Their country no longer serves its people, but rather only its perpetrators. When the United States still stood for something, it had a saying too. It went, "Truth, Justice and the American Way". Regrettably that's now been transformed into, "Sleuth, Just Us and the Americans Slay".

"Oversight and accountability" are other important ingredients to preserving a healthy nation, but I have no right or authority to tell you how that might be applied to Russia's unique government structure. It is not for me to say. A grave and permanent damage was done to the American system in its lack of oversight and slowly decoupling from its foundational ideals and principles. With this came the burgeoning and behemoth corporate monopolies, crushing the unique and rare, regional start-up businesses and cultures beneath the wheel. The society forever lost its authentic character, its charm and charisma in that it no longer saw its people in its reflection, but rather only the shadows of a degenerative, non-benevolent, toxic, franchising, self-serving and corrupt, corporate cesspool.

I believe that to be eclectic in the sense that one can adopt small, specific aspects, practices and methods from something which can greatly benefit you, while discarding the remaining parts, is often a wise approach. Learning from other's mistakes too, can many times offer you immediate opportunities, by avoiding to make them yourself.

Even though I might express a distaste for corporations in the "monopolies" sense, I do not feel them all to be delinquent. Sometimes a corporation can be compared to an individual and in doing so, one might discover some advantages and even qualities worth aspiring to. In my book Tandem there is interpreted research taken from a 1983 Royal Dutch Shell Corp. (RDS) study. The core reason I attempt to share these valuable aspects of both empires and corporations is because I would like to see Russia not only succeed, but to maintain and develop an inherent set of practices which could enable it to actually intervene history, avoid all the pitfalls that lead to demise and prove to past history that it is possible not to become a fallen empire.

To achieve this in a perpetual sense requires not only to never forget to remind one's self to re-study the reasons of those who have fallen before you, but to always aspire to pressure and enhance Russia's commercial and ascending prosperity with an intelligence which never permits itself to become too affluent and disconnected from its core values and ideals.

For instance, perhaps if society were required to somehow re-live the empire's pioneering and conquest stages (minus the wars), every time it was soon approaching thee affluent and intellect stages, "decadence and decline" might be avoided. In some way, humankind must seek to develop methods capable of intercepting the repetition of rise-and-fall. This sounds absurd at first, but no country has ever tried it before. Since every empire in existence has eventually fallen, isn't it at least worth considering in the theoretical sense, a new hybrid approach to intervening history to avoid catastrophe?

If a new empire were to somehow hybridize this concept and couple it with RDS's findings of "the leading characteristics of the longest surviving companies" (700 years or more), perhaps we might attain an infinite solution for an empire to actually experience a "perpetual longevity". The leading characteristics for the RDS study were:

- Sensitivity to their environment

- Cohesiveness, with a strong sense of identity

- Tolerance, except for centralized control. Respect for eccentricity.

- Conservative finance. Surpluses preferred over indebtedness.

Mixing and combining all of these ingredients with a new hybridized approach to addressing the different stages of an empire, sounds like a very fascinating concept which might pan out the secret to a perpetual empire; "Russia forever"! One thing I must stipulate here. This whole approach I have mentioned should only be considered by working with your existing country's government structure already in place and then possibly modifying or implementing measures when needed over time. I am not condoning "social experiments", "forced culture shock", or revolutions!

    Another alternative to help reset and hybridize a nation's existence for perpetual centuries might start with always making the domestic economy a priority. To compare corporations that are 700 years old or more, those corporations never used to preoccupy themselves with quarterly profits, only the overall general health of the entire host. Believe it or not, there once was a law on the books in America which required all publicly-held companies to "cease and desist" after a 50 to 70 year period. After that time the company would be entirely liquated and the proceeds of all total assets were distributed amongst the shareholders. This is just more food for thought, in terms of coming up with a variety of trace elements to feed a society for longevity. As for the domestic economy being a priority, it only stands to reason that a country that can survive without being dependent for its survival, only makes it more capable of remaining independent. The United States of today is now very inter-dependent.

"Intervention"; how do we interrupt the tides of history to prevent an empire from going the way as all those before it? Well for one, it starts with people warming-up to the idea that it even might be possible. After this it takes awareness, another trait to long survival. Always to remain aware of what's happening and to your environment without becoming complacent. The key moment in time that has been pin-pointed by all historians and researchers of what makes empires fall is "the arrival of the affluent stage". Once more and more money begins to change hands and the general quality of life in the society begins to rise, therein is the exact place in time to take action, if you want to be a nation most unique to any other before your time.

Affluence promotes luxury, detachment, a hedonistic separation from the foundational principles of a culture. It invites corruption, greed, an infiltration to morality, ethics and discipline. This then is followed by the "intellect age" where people become more liberal and lost in their thinking, to a point where they give patriotism no attention and begin to feel as if they are superior to their founding fathers and their principles which laid the foundation to the culture.

The reason Russians should never take history too lightly can be best appreciated by paying close attention to the many examples of America's decline today. In 2012 alone, the U.S. introduced 40,000 new laws. Today it could half-jokingly be said that it is a place where "everything is illegal", if one were to get technical. As America came out of its "Affluent stage" and thrashed into its "age of intellect", its practice of multiculturalism was instigated by its silent perpetrators systemically who I might add, are descendants of the same people who instigated Russia's Bolshevik Revolution. They introduced multiculturalism into American society to destabilize it, dilute it and to weaken it. Suddenly it found itself not with new immigrants who had any interest in actually becoming Americans, only citizens for a passport to gain welfare benefits and to "transplant" their culture which they brought with them.

So remember you must first, never accept a coup, you question more, shun multiculturalism that is to say, it is positive to respect and learn about other cultures, but it is a self-dividing force if a nation permits more than one culture to be practiced as a replacement to the existing one, as opposed to being a much stronger melting pot which fuses many into one unity. "Limits on wealth". Do you think we should have them? It has never really been seriously discussed inside a democratic free society. It is just another one of my foods for thought. Conceptually it would mean something like, say we set a figure of $10 million US dollars as the most anyone were ever permitted to be worth, anything more and it would have to go back into the society in some way or form.

Edward Gibbons, a writer of enormous, historic proportions, between 1776 and 1788 authored a six volume set of books, in which the subject matter spanned some 1,200 years. It was known as "The

History of the Decline and Fall of the Roman Empire". Gibbons too targets "luxury" as the epidemic virus which eventually takes all empires down. In his work he named eight primary causes for the Roman Empire's extinction:

- A decline in morals and values

- A decline in public health quality

- Political corruption

- Unemployment *(caused by wealthy men)

- Inflation *(caused by deficits and over-reliance upon the State)

- Urban decay *(caused by the wealthy's destruction of the middle class)

- Inferior Technology *(caused by a very narrow spectrum)

- Military Spending *(caused by over-expansionism and an over-reliance on mercenary forces)

     In learning from others' mistakes as you know, the United States has now entered into its "age of Decadence and Decline", sometime during these past three decades. Nearing the brink of oppression and destruction, over the past 28 years of its presidential administrations and congresses, its liberal ideologists and neoconservative extremists have melded the republic into an identical predicament as Hitler's, that is to say, "a state of perpetual war". During this age it has proceeded to make enemies with 75% of the planet's nations while it currently begins setting its sights on "its very own people". Again, the very same decedents of America's perpetrators who took part in its coup, are not only one and the same with those who caused the Bolshevik Revolution, but Germany's upheavals as well.

Quite similar to a banana republic, U.S. law enforcement intelligence agencies are currently being conditioned to treat American citizens as an enemy, while stoking its prison system with more political prisoners than true criminals. A bit like, "the criminals locking up the law abiding ones". I'm forced into portraying America in this way, due to the fact that G.W. Bush, Dick Cheney and Hillary Clinton have yet to be incarcerated, while they enjoy a lifestyle much like ancient kings and queens. As I write this, all of Washington's bureaucrats seem to be drunk on power and personal ambitions. They have completely disconnected from their duties of serving the people as representatives.

In less than another decade American citizens will find themselves under a more openly severe and oppressive regime – a Fascist State. Russia however, has many advantages. It has never encouraged mass multicultural immigration. It has already survived a Jewish extremist genocide. It is a strong Christian nation. It has already tried and abandoned various social experiments and over-bearing, socioeconomic restraints. In rather sharp contrast, America is currently a runaway train with a bourgeoisie unchecked in affluent corruption and white collar criminality.

Once removed by Reagan and Gorbachev, America's one-and-the-same liberal ideologists' and neoconservatives' psychotic policies towards China and Russia have now resurrected the threat of nuclear Armageddon. America is now Newmerika; an Israeli colony fully controlled by very demented, psychotic, psychopathic criminal gluttons.

They have incubated from a fully hatched pandemic as a malicious contagion stretching from Tel Aviv on through to its Washington puppets and vassal Euro-lapdogs States. On a daily basis they pipeline an over pressurized, combustible hegemony throughout the geopolitical landscape. Never forget that you are not dealing with America anymore, but "Newmerika", America's hijackers, coup perpetrators and warmongering instigators, all of whom act completely on their own and out of the control of the American people themselves. They no longer act as representatives of the government, but as dictators telling the people who will be their president, even when the majority of the voting public refuses their candidates.

They entrap government officials in various ways. Sometimes they drug them then put them into compromising situations such as being photographed with a prostitute, or with a tax issue, an insider trading issue and sometimes even plain death threats. The truth is in the numbers. Only 9% of Americans surveyed approve of their government, while the #1 cause of death among U.S. soldiers is now "suicide". Soldiers are openly ordered to protect poppy fields in Afghanistan just to support the world's heroine supply. Am I getting through to you, just how far gone the former United States is today?

Need I remind you, what we have here are the creators, designers and assemblers of terrorism itself. They are "the devil cornered", so you might imagine the highly volatile desperation you are dealing with. At this juncture it will try anything, as witnessed in its attempts to undermine the Minsk Agreements, its refusal of cooperation with Russia, Assad, China and a legitimate MH-17 investigation, as well as in its false claims and sabotaged evidence to instigate sanctions, while it attempts to fully destabilize Europe, not Russia.

This menacing Newmerikan-Israeli Zionist monster, neocon-liberal ideological Frankenstein serpent of a Washingtonian Crime Cabal will openly slither across all boundaries of the law, including blackmail, extortion, torture and murder, regardless of if you are an individual, or member of the IMF (International Monetary Fund). That's right, the IMF has now literally had a gun put to its head, to be made a tool for Newmerika's foreign policy agenda.

These actions stated now make all Western law, institutions, policies, contracts, markets and even currency absolutely meaningless and unquestionably illegitimate. All of them now hold no legal premise, standing by no stable set of ideals and are completely absent of any ethics or oversight. All of Western civilization has just destroyed its last, final forms of any "legal and authentic identity". It has now been completely hollowed out and fully liquidated. Nothing more than a looting mechanism with nuclear warheads remains. Its people don't want war, but they are no longer permitted to object to it. Remember, 55% of Newmerikans now take some form of anti-depressants.

Severely wealthy, homicidal psychopaths have completely taken the West under control. These days the devil is a very desperate man. His money is now worthless and all that he has left is a chance to start a war that he knows he cannot win (West vs China-Russia). Will he self-destruct quietly, or will he make an attempt to have us join him in Armageddon and the destruction of all life?

Be forewarned, there are these circumstances only and one variable chance that he will attempt to terrorize "any" section of the non-Western alliance he can manage. You have passed the point of any reconciliation, or possible peaceful agreement with this creature. Your only option in dealing with it may require to completely exclude the beast from any and all association. At this juncture it may be the only options to the total annihilation of all life. To permit the beast no-entry into anywhere, or anything in non-Western regions, until it is left with nothing more than to devour its own people. Trust me, better them than you. We had our chance and nobody stepped forward, while most just proceeded to stick their heads in the sand.

Islamic scholar and global affairs analyst Shaykh Imran Hosein stated, "We must expose and prosecute them now, or drown in blood". He made this statement to the False Flag Islamophobia Conference and is predicting an avalanche of false-flags on the heels of the San Bernardino and Paris shooting incidents.

U.S. whistleblower and former NSA/CIA contractor. Steven D. Kelly has exposed "Craft International", the same entity which bombed the Boston Marathon, as the true author of the San Bernardino mass murders. This is far removed from anything that America's founding fathers had chartered and this is not what America is supposed to be about. It was never intended to be a Jewish-owned media-springboard of hate and misleading propaganda against Muslims people, or as a forum for whipping up hysterical lies to go to war against China and Russia. Why is no one talking about Israel? It actually makes complete logical sense to go to war against Israel. It makes no convincing or logical sense to go to war against Russia or China, or to hate Muslim people.

What greatly cheats the Russian people in this chapter is that I had fully intended it to be devoted, solely to contributing various forms of advice that could possibly assist their "peace-loving", civil and ethical society. But now, due to the gross negligence of Western rulers' recent actions in constantly flirting with variable chances of sparking a nuclear war - they are beating Newmerikans' heads silly for them to go to war. This forces me to devote too much time, thought and space to discussing "Western pro-war idioms", rather than the issues normally facing a sane and peacefully co-existing world. I guess the repercussions of Newmerika's destabilization has managed to even make ripples as I try to write this.

Newmerika is pushing policies that are geared to an end to all life, whether ironic or paradoxical. Washington shall find itself in deep trouble, once China deciphers the writing on the wall. The Western, Jewish hate-criminals of its presstitude news networks, along with their extorted Washington puppets, completely avoid all logical questioning and are proving to be the most blood-thirsty commercial components in this American society under siege.

Newmerikans and Europeans (or in this case, Euro-peed-ons') history shall write, if there's ever anyone left remaining to read it, that they made a unanimous choice to surrender their sovereign duties to uphold and defend justice, in the eyes of their God, in the eyes of the Law and in the eyes of their own grandmothers' and chose rather, to cower and hide with their heads stuck deep inside the matrix, sucking their thumbs while they waited for reality to just hopefully go away.

Everything that Reagan and Gorbachev worked for has been cast to the winds by Israel's psychopath Newmerika who's blood-letting, eye-popping lust for hegemony over the world now hangs in the balance of life's final and last breaths. To deliver such a wonderful and beautiful world into complete annihilation is the most sinful of all waste.

But I and all good people of the Earth will rather die happily standing, than to live a life on our knees in such a dastardly, demented world, of these sickened tormentors.

The devil can't win and so rather than face surrender he is taking the world hostage in the hopes of starting a nuclear war, where he might stand a chance of taking all of us with him. He is no worse than the millions of cowardice Europeans and Newmerikans who do nothing.

Life was great. It was undermined by lies as it will be ended by lies. Like the expert said, "It only takes one mistake and 30 minutes to destroy life on Earth". I will pray to every God, including Muslims', that every evil doer in the West's hegemony shall some morning cease to exist and that we may receive a divine intervention of 1,000 years of peace.

Chapter V

Newmerika's Choice

A well renowned and accomplished musician and lyricist who went by the stage name of "Taj Mahal" once said, "Come with me, leave your yesterdays, your yesterdays behind and take a giant step outside your mind" (from his song, "Giant Step").

The constant daily exposure to late-breaking, technological gizmos, gadgetry and daily new technological applications, runs counter to the act of adherence. If possible, at least outside one's workplace, grant yourself a years' vacation from smartphones, any major news networks, Clear Channel Corporate broadcasting and Murdoch NewsCorp publications. Check-in to a $15 barebones cell phone and don't go on the internet for more than six hours-a-week. You may even consider leaving your phone at home once in a while.

My perception to "taking a giant step outside one's mind", is to reach, get in touch with, nurture and replenish your "organic self"; your innermost, truthful identity.

Nature has taught us that a key to a healthy survival requires not only a development and conditioning of routine methods, systems and procedures, it also demands loyalty, consistency and reliable cohesion. When one becomes too caught up in updating their apps, this is anti-cohesive. It constantly destroys a loyalty to one's own methods and systems and replaces any cohesiveness with a wishy-washy sense of "here today, gone tomorrow". To remain loyal to a given set of methods, systems and routines that works best for you, is not to be archaic, outdated, or ole-fashioned, it is to be connected to a sense of longevity, the longest and healthiest measure of survivability.

For one to over-fuss, or waste too much precious time updating their Facebook page, is not organic expression, it is window-dressing your public relations to a digital world which is not real. Rather, it is a temporary exhilaration of your ego's emotions. It is not even cosmic, but digital. Pie in the sky, sensory doodling.

What makes proven corporations prevail for more than 700 years are the same things which enable healthy individuals to live 100 years. Yes they can be fun, open to reasonable change and even be innovative and pioneering. But they both remain loyal to a proven set of laws, culture, procedures, principles, methods, morality, systems and even styles, which strengthens and invigorates their health and longevity. One of the biggest concerns within what remains of the Western world today, is the large scale difficulty in getting people of their society to "focus and live for a brief moment in the present tense". It can baffle one's mind to observe just how much of their populations never grants themselves a considerable chance to actually see, live and breathe life as it exists in the present moment and unfolding. This is similar to a locomotive engineer racing down a set of rails, coupled to boxcars of "the past", while he looks out with anticipating eyes to what's ahead, yet completely neglects to ever look down at his or her gauges, or to make the necessary adjustments for pressures, fuel and breakage.

Western societies have no leadership and this is now trickling down to every human resource department of every one of their corporations. It starts with "the State", their governments. Right now their governments have no leaders, no examples of ethical, law-abiding, principled individuals. Their present majority is unethical, above the law and corrupt. They no longer can get responsible people elected and so they remain stuck with nothing more than bought-and-paid-for millionaires on a string. Akin to puppet dictators one could say, who run recklessly over their people's consensus and basically administer what their constituency's' agenda orders them to. They are as detached from truth and justice as the devil is from heaven.

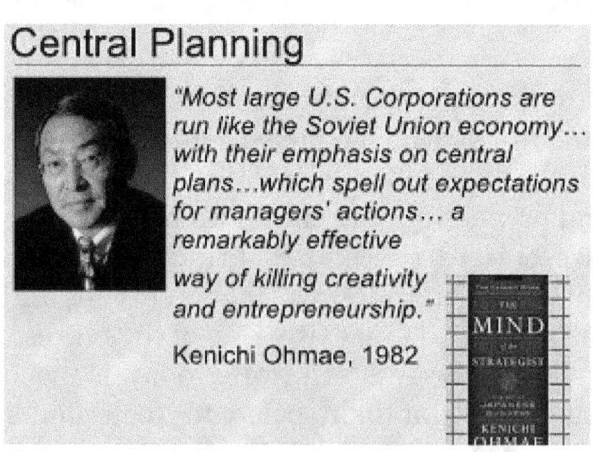

Central Planning

"Most large U.S. Corporations are run like the Soviet Union economy... with their emphasis on central plans...which spell out expectations for managers' actions... a remarkably effective way of killing creativity and entrepreneurship."

Kenichi Ohmae, 1982

Newmerikans live in "The New Totalitarianism". They've permitted their corporations to make America like the old Soviet Union. Their savior was supposed to be "free market capitalism", to defend them from the tyranny of faceless apparatchiks, but that's not what happened. The twentieth century power struggle between

Soviet-styled communism and free-market capitalism was for domination of the world's resources. Though Newmerika assumed that Soviet communism lost, China's more capitalist strain seems to be doing just fine. Newmerika's corporatism took for granted that its superiority affirmed once and for all that its neo-liberal economics were destined to be top dog.

A funny thing happened on the way to the forum with this, though. The old adage, "Know your enemy, you may become a lot like him" slowly reared its ugly head. The Kafkaesque attributes of the Soviet system have found their ways into noxious policies and practices of Newmerika's victorious corporations. Much like the unhappy citizenry in those old, centrally planned USSR economies, Newmerika's corporations too often now leave their employees, customers and other stakeholders, just as powerless over their own fate.

One should think it to be awful enough that they've taken control over the U.S. government, however they seemed to have also consumed Newmerika's choices in what they buy, where they work, how they live and what rights they still have. Newmerikan's quality of life has now deteriorated to an extent of being determined by Politburo apparatchiks, much like a Supreme Corporate Soviet some place, only now their called PR-men, marketing executives, icons of corporate finance, lobbyists for multinationals and bean-counting managers trying to increase quarterly profits at Newmerikan's expense of their freedoms.

Soviet-style, corporate overlords have run their brigades of tanks over a once, very "wealth-sharing" society. Mom and Pop stores used to distribute goods from a wide variety of small, "domestic" manufacturers. They also produced a very sizeable amount of middle class jobs and an immense variety of retail choices. Main street stores were dotted with a full spectrum of selections which were supported by numerous different suppliers. Small merchants competed to set their brands apart and the styles and goods would change and reflect more of the local cultures, as one travelled from region to region.

Newmerika's stores today are "Big-box, Supreme Soviet" on parade. Choices are limited and the same junk on their shelves and hangers in New Jersey are identical to the ones in Montana. Nowhere are there reflections of the local culture, unless you pay for "upscale boutique" goods which are more often than not, owned by some Politburo Chief's wife as a "tax-dodge hobby". Communities too have been replaced by "the Mall". Yes and even Newmerika's own water is sold back to them by Pepsi and Coke. Wal-mart now sells 25% of Newmerika's groceries, so if one can't find their variety of preference you're out of luck, since the local grocers have all gone out of business.

In the advent of online shopping, one of Newmerika's severe squeezing of choice can be seen in its media stores. The limited shelf space of big box behemoths are still the largest purchasers of toys and video games. For more than two decades this aspect has dominated the decision-making process of both businesses. Should the shoppers at Wal-mart not like your product, manufacturers won't even consider making it. Not only that, but Wal-mart operates at some blood-letting, thin profit margins meaning suppliers are forced into a high-volume, thinly priced environment where they can be made toast of in an instant.

This Soviet-styled, centralized control in markets possesses no "free-market" style thinking, when a select few buyers at Wal-mart headquarters dictates what products will be made available. Having less choice and variety in their market places is Newmerika's corporatization of its consumer landscape. This old Soviet-styled, centralized planning in Newmerika's heavily franchised chain stores has robbed it from being enabled to reflect any sort of character, local flavor, rarity or quality. One could even go so far as to say, it sometimes appears that 50% of anything offered in Newmerika's marketplace, was made with Homer Simpson in mind. The resulting bland, fran-cheesy, Disneyfied choices in entertainment, ideas and experiences, are far removed from the creative, genuine town and country feel of neighborhood stores gone by.

Herein lies the irony, when Newmerika's "free market" proclamations have now stooped to one and the same level of old, Soviet-styled, poorly stocked, State controlled storefronts. Newmerika's shoppers are finally seeming to be getting some relief though, in the onset of online shopping. The country's big-box stores and malls have caused this backlash, due in part to its "Sovietization" of the free-market system, yet the "culture" itself still lays destroyed. I say this since "community" was displaced and replaced by "the digital community" which is still a buzzword for "no community". But at least local producers are getting back into the act, much thanks to technology. I for one am a living example having taken full advantage of the advent in online, on-demand self-publishing.

The kind of healthcare Newmerikans get when they can get it, has taken it on the chin from the Supreme Health Care Soviet. Doctors with independent practices have been swept away, along with choice and selection, by the thundering undertow of the Profit Politburo. The administrative costs of dealing with Newmerika's Soviet-styled bureaucrats has forced 2/3's of its primary care physicians to surrender their practices. They've been swallowed into the belly of the beast, as just another salaried, corporate employee that is forced under pressure to shorten visits, pad billable hours, adhere to narrow procedures and shoot patients through like cattle fodder in harvest.

Requiring doctors to put in extra hours, its insurance accountants seem to second-guess every claim while forcing them into a revolving door, writing letters and making calls to defend their patient's rights to care. Pharmaceutical giant's co-op each channel of information doctors rely on for new drugs and treatments, from peer-reviewed journals to medical conferences, to the drug information inserts. In undermining evidence-based medicine, big pharma Profit Politburo ensures that doctors won't ever get important information that has the potential to affect the sales of profitable drugs, driving a corporate – Lysenkoism to prevail.

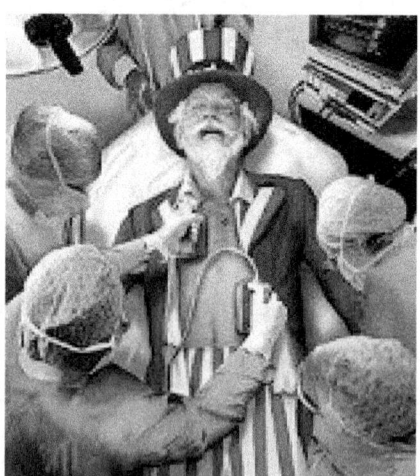

Many States in Newmerika are passing laws which invite them into the examination rooms, passing laws for stipulation for what doctors can and cannot tell their patients about their own condition. Newmerika's old style, Soviet medical Politburo, in some cases even oversteps the USSR era by having State medical lawyers demand doctors to flat out lie to patients, for reasons entirely unrelated to scientific medicine and more in line with political correctness. Politburo apparatchiks at Newmerikans' employer corporate headquarters, decide entirely what a patient deserves to have in this co-opted macabre of compromised care. Layers of centralized interference from officials who are not qualified MDs, block the liberties of a patient-doctor relationship and often greatly influence the decision-making processes. I'm not talking government interference here; in order to draw profits from both the doctors and their patients, "corporate" interests subjugate them to a centralized regime. This is what Newmerikas were told Soviet medicine was like, during the first Cold War.

Newmerikans have now switched places with Russia. While Vladimir Putin's Russia now stands for "truth, justice and a free-market system", Newmerika adopts the regimented, overly-managed and central control of the old Cold War Sovietization and it will cost them more than anywhere else on the entire planet.

Newmerika's teachers used to be famous for telling their students startling tall tales concerning their unlucky peers in the USSR. They use to profess that Communist education was completely void of debate, critical thinking and variety, while being undermined by high-stakes tests scores which would eventually assess one student's place in Party hierarchy. They used fearmongering Newmerika's students that their Soviet counterparts weren't permitted to freely choose their professions or consider their own interests. They were led to believe Soviet students were sorted like potatoes, tracked to serve the desires of the State and were not treated as individuals. All decisions were dictated by a central authority they were told and a determination as to what type of workers were needed by the State and what schools students had to be assigned to would be made.

The enormous ironies by comparisons continually boggles the mind. While Newmerika was giving up on encouraging critical thinking and creativity in its onboarding students, China was picking up on them and implementing the concepts into its curriculums. Over the past 150 years, in a manner only a Soviet bureaucrat could love, Newmerika's educational systems have been favoring centralized, test-driven regimes in schooling, while surrendering their competitive edge. Just as the best schools in the USSR were reserved for the children of Party leadership, so too in present day Newmerika do the higher echelons of its society inherit the majority of opportunities to the best high schools and universities. To make matters even more atrocious for Newmerikan students, "for-profit" corporations have succeeded in hijacking their education from the hands of the State. And so it continues that in the case of Newmerikan life today, the more one reads old stories describing the horrors once associated with Soviet life, the more closely they are describing its old Cold War foe in the present tense.

If you care for more evidence, just consider the following:

- Large, Soviet-style developers are over-seeing modern housing projects designed by market researchers that dictate what "The People's Houses" should look like.

- Soviet-styled, government mandated (but privately ran) monocultures dominate Newmerika's foods supply.

- "Corporate owned" machines count Newmerika's votes. Much like the use to limit Communist Party membership to a small percentage of the population, Newmerika's voting system is increasingly restricted to people who are acceptable to the party hierarchy.

- Newmerika now has gulags identical to the old Soviet policing styles that are run by corporations as a militarized law enforcement.

- Lysenkoism of a Newmerikan science-denial movement is flexing its response to climate change. It seems any demands made on corporations to change their ways is the main fundraiser.

- What was once the stuff of totalitarian nightmares, the faceless and inhumane bureaucracy is now found in Newmerika's bank foreclosures. Checks and papers vanish, payments are never posted and the runarounds given to their consumers is an ordeal that could roll over even Franz Kafka's eyes.

Newmerika's masses are footing a huge expense for this corporate-sponsored tyranny. During the past 60 years, Newmerika's politicians pounded the tables of debate for free-markets and resistance to Communism. What it ended up with is a world that feels and acts more like the very entity it sought to oppose. In what now resembles a centrally planned hell hole, corporate overlords raped and pillaged Newmerika's resources and energy only to fund and erect the very monster beast of totalitarianism they campaigned against.

Though the USSR has been dead and buried for 20 years, die-hard anti-communists still go feverishly on the lookout, glued to their T.V. sets to updates for any signs of government-inflicted socialism or lone wolf totalitarians. Unbeknownst to these tin foil hats, their scouting in the wrong direction. In actuality the genuine liberty-stripping, dignity-destroying, soul-squishing oppressors are coming from not the government, but the corporations they once held as their shining shields against the Communist invaders.

The centrally planned authoritarian State they've always feared has already arrived. The government can no longer protect and defend them from the power-hungry businesses anymore. They're now well established for the privately, for-profit few and without a spec of resistance from those ardent tin foil hats who've been standing watch for years, swearing it could never happen to them. Free from the pesky principles of accountability and oversight, that same old monster has already consumed them under a brand new skin.

If you are Newmerikan, some of the brightest sellouts afforded by the New World Order (NWO) ghouls has been to massively promote polished versions of their billion dollar product for years. You're not listening to your outer and inner warnings to move beyond it is your only shame. Unilateral neocons (neoconservatives) and ideologs, (ideologists) along with the financial analysts, psychologists and sociologists, have been busy trying to erect their superstructure. The globalist minions, through institutes such as "Tavistock" and Stanford Research Institute (SRI), have been attempting to shape the thinking of the masses in formulations to hopefully make them more NWO-compatible.

The Tavistock Institute was best described by Lord Bertrand Russell who revealed some of the Frankfurt Schools' most profound principles, in his 1951 book, "The Impact of Science on Society", as follows: "I think the subject which will be most important politically is mass psychology..., its importance has been enormously increased by the growth of modern methods of propaganda. Of these, the most influential is what is called 'education'. Religion plays a part, though a diminishing one; the press, the cinema and radio play an increasing part..., it may be hoped that in time, anybody will be able to persuade anybody of anything, if he can catch the patient young and is provided by the State with money and equipment".

"Although this science will be diligently studied, it will be rigidly confined to the governing class. The populace will not be allowed to know how its convictions were generated. When the technique has been perfected, every government that has been in charge of education for a generation, will be able to control its subject securely, without the need of armies or policemen". Notice how nonchalantly Russell assumes that "control of the masses" is his God-given right, assumed as a worthwhile phenomenon.

In 1946 The Rockefeller Foundation, using a grant separate from the Tavistock Clinic, formed its own group known as the Tavistock Insitute of Human Relations. These groups were just some of the budding examples of the "secret societies" U.S. President Kennedy was attempting to alert the public to. A former British Intelligence Agent John Coleman, explained that the Rockefeller version had Tavistock designed methods and was responsible for what got the U.S. into World War II. He also pointed out that, under a Dr. Kurt Lewin's guidance it established the OSS, later known as the CIA.

In Britain when it came to psychoanalysis and the psychodynamic or Freud theories, Tavistock became known as the focal point. Tavistock takes a peculiar and interesting twist. On the surface, Tavistock seems innocent enough, portraying itself as a British charity involved with group and organizational behavior, but here's where the snowball really gets rolling. Its trail begins as research and consultancy work in social sciences and applied psychology, engaged in education. Upon closer examination of its clientele, they include public sector organizations such as the European Union, some British government departments and networks stretching from the University of Sussex to Newmerika's Silicon Valley with Stanford Research Institute (SRI), Esalen Institute, MIT, Hudson Institute, Brookings Institution, Aspen Institute, the Heritage Foundation, the Center of Strategic and International Studies at Georgetown, U.S. Airforce Intelligence and the RAND Corporation.

A predominantly "Jewish group of philosophers and Marxist theorists", who fled Germany when Hitler shutdown their "Institut fur Sozialforschung" (Institute for Social Research) at the University of Frankfurt, the Tavistock Institute's projects were a follow-up on the work done by them at that university. Focusing on the study and criticism of culture developed from the thought of Freud, the school's main figures sought to learn from and fuse the works of such varied thinkers as Kant, Hegel, Marx, Freud, Weber and Lukacs. One can begin to see a pattern surface in their involvement with the development of Newmerika's 1960's drug counterculture and the CIA mind control techniques, through SRI

(Stanford Research Institute), of Menlo Park, then located just across the street from today's Facebook headquarters.

Tavistock Institute Of Human Relations: Shaping the Moral, Spiritual, Cultural, Political, and Economic Decline of The United States of America.

While he was a student at Stanford University in nearby Palo Alto, California, "Merry Prankster" Ken Kesey, author of "One Flew Over the Cuckoo's Nest," volunteered for some "MK Ultra" experiments which involved the partaking of LSD and other psychedelic drugs at the Veterans Administration Hospital in Menlo Park. What greatly influenced the "hippie culture" of the 1960's were Kesey's promotion of LSD, which were heavily influenced by its effects on him through these sponsored experiments. It also becomes evident that today's "Facebook" will play a major role in the undermining of the next generation.

So it is here, where we can first begin to locate the origins of Newmerika's failed, "New World Order" ideology. Through this act of "destabilization" and "control" over a 50 year period (1965 – 2015) these predominantly Marxist-Leninist organizations have guided their "peace and love" experiments through a transformation into "hate and fear" campaigns through their creation of "terrorism", destabilization and destruction. They are responsible for all of Newmerika's illicit drug problems and the campaign of hate against Russia, as if the 66 million already killed during the Bolshevik Revolution by their affiliates of these organizations wasn't enough.

A Newmerikan lyricist, singer-songwriter, translator and poet, Robert Hunter, whose popularity rose during his associations with the rock band "The Grateful Dead", joined Kesey as a subject in the MK Ultra experiments at Stanford University. These "paid" subjects were to report their experiences and side-effects after having been administered an assortment of LSD, psilocybin and mescaline.

What you the reader needs to understand is that all which I am discovering and interpreting for you describes not only most reader's "enemy", but Vladimir Putin's as well. It is my own personal style that I have chosen in this chapter, to better illustrate just what exactly Mr. Putin is up against. And it is quite a fickle twist of irony that we learn here that the "true destroyers of the United States" are actually one and the same enemy to not only Newmerikans, but to Russians and Chinese and over half the free world.

Alfred Lambremont Webre, an alumni of Stanford Research Institute (SRI), has been very active in the alternative media. To follow, decipher and interpret such an individual gets extra-tricky, as these Tavistock oriented individuals all seem to possess a very intricate form of insanity. What's even more bizarre are the governments (including Newmerika's) which actually have hired these tin foil hats to implement ideals, visions, ideologies and agendas, both one and the same as Marxist-Leninist rabble-rousers and that runs counter to the very democratic principles the governments who hire them, stand for.

Hence, as was the case with "peace and love" being slowly manifested as "hate and destruction", what you at first see more often than not with these people (Tavistock followers), turns out to be the opposite in the end. After numerous attempts to study and assess Mr. Webre, I was forced to conclude that he mixes bits of the truth with decoy-like deception. In my own evaluations I would classify Alfred Webre as a Tavistock Institute for Human Relations mole inside the realm of alternative media, who serves as a double-agent sent to mildly discuss some of the simple truths surrounding the old New World Order mind control, but done in a manner to act as a decoy. What this purpose serves is a duality in and of itself. He firstly states issues cast in an anti-NWO light of description, but done in such a way as to greatly defuse the awakening against it, while his actions are simultaneously serving as sort of a Pied Piper form of identifying "the awakened". One thing I have learned for certain is that the new generations had better wake up quickly to the use of "Facebook", as it is my analysis this venue has incredibly dire and evil consequences for the future of its members. In the end it will prove to be one hellish chronic bane, capable of both completely ruining many member's lives, while branding them for life, much like the tattooed serial numbers on inmates of concentration camps. These I have concluded are its main objectives.

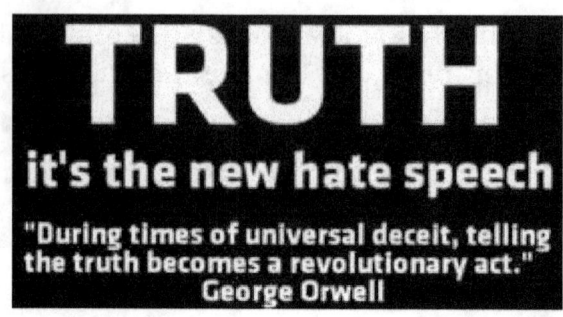

TRUTH
it's the new hate speech
"During times of universal deceit, telling
the truth becomes a revolutionary act."
George Orwell

Another alternative media figure accused of using deception is
Alex Jones. I have not studied the man enough to make a clear case
for this, but he is known for his alternative news venues and again,
this "Pied Piper" contingency method of "tag-and-identify" keeps
coming up among his critics. As for Alfred Lambremont Webre I
have relayed in notes from a Vancouver, British Columbia interview
with him: "In 1977 he joined Stanford Research Institute
International in Menlo Park, California as a futurist for the Center
for the Study of Social Policy. His responsibilities were the studies
in alternative futures, innovation diffusion and social policy
applications for clients, including the Carter White House's
Extraterrestrial Communications Study, The National Science
Foundation, the U.S. Congress Office of Technology Assessment,
the U.S. Department of Energy and the State of California Energy
Plan."

Having experience in dreaming up "alternative futures",
Webre has applied this experience within the mind-screw of the
alternative realms, as he imposes them upon the awakening masses.
The dramatically deep canyons of discontentment and psychopathic
dementia which afflicts these individuals such as Webre bears
evidence that though he and his constituency all possess a capacity
in education, wealth and experience which would enable them to
enjoy a perfectly wonderful life, they rather choose to dedicate it to
concocting schemes of robbery, control, pain and suffering upon the

masses, for the benefit of an elite few. In an "Informed Planet" – "News Inside Out" interview with J.F. Simard, Webre speaks of a new planetary age of individual sovereignty and a BRICS Golden Age. He makes mention of a holographic timeline that activated near December 21, 2012 which he predicts will transform a planned 2015 financial collapse of the U.S. Federal Reserve Bank fiat Petrodollar.

This has been interpreted by other futurists to being not only unsuccessful (or late in coming), but a functional component of a Jesuit – Matrix depopulation plan, better known as "The Great Culling", which includes Fukushima radiation, GMOs, Vaccines, Geo-engineering, Wars, planned financial collapse and a Mad Max type of Ascension into the Transhumanist Agenda, which is claimed to no longer be operative in our time – space hologram. Webre's interview refers to an "evil Anglo-American elite" which is **"decoy #1".** There is no "Anglo American elite". Though there once was, as it began to share power with the then Zionist – Jewish coalition in the planning and aftermath of the Kennedy Assassination, the WASP overlords have been finding themselves under the thumb of their former partners ever since.

Webre then makes mention of this factious WASP elite being in association with "Draco Reptilian aliens who have a penchant for human sushi"! This is **"decoy #2".** There are no aliens. It has already been proven that UFOs were first invented by the "Vril Society" of Germany with their success being predominately attributed to one Victor Schauberger. Their first successful anti-gravitational craft, the RSB-2 performed its first maiden flight in 1934 and can be seen in my prior book "Tandem" on page 108 of chapter three. (Note: The craft on the page following it is an animation). You will notice throughout my history in writing I never once buy-into the conspiracy theory of "alien beings" from outer space. "Majestic" or MJ-12, the super-secret panel that William Cooper, former Naval Intelligence Officer turned whistle blower often referred to, seemed always being more concerned with "cover-ups" and using disinformation. They demonstrated repeated attempts to keep both the concept of alien space creatures and the whole UFO mystique alive in people's minds in order to deflect from the fact that there actually is an elitist "human" group of internationalists who possess these crafts confiscated from Germany at the end of WW II. They likely have since been reengineered, upgraded and produced. This Western brand of style Webre attempts to roll out is identical to what William Cooper often mentioned as the elite's knack for having several programs or plots running simultaneously, one of which was "the concept of aliens" who, in a false-flag operation would make it appear that alien forces from space were attacking earth, in an attempt to force the New World Order to jell into formation.

Crazy Al (Alfred Lambremont Webre) then makes claims that this "evil Anglosphere is trying to kill everybody", which is **decoy #3"**. White Anglo Saxons aren't trying to kill anybody, it's the Zionist-Jewish Cabal who are backing the killing wars, media-hate campaigns and division of the masses. This statement however, is very significant in that it's the first time the upper crust has broken from the traditional stencil mold of blaming everything bad on the Muslims. For the elites to start talking about "the Anglos" means that they now want them completely booted out of the power structure. This is all purely Marxist-Leninist trickery plain and simple, used to deflect blame and afford them an entity to hide behind. When they were gangsters in "Murder Inc." they hid behind and blamed Italians, when they were terrorists in the USS Liberty Incident and the 9-11 Incident they hid behind Muslims, now they want to up-the-ante and go for an exclusively Zionist-Jewish elite and hide behind the Anglos. It's all about "deflecting their own blame onto anyone else but themselves".

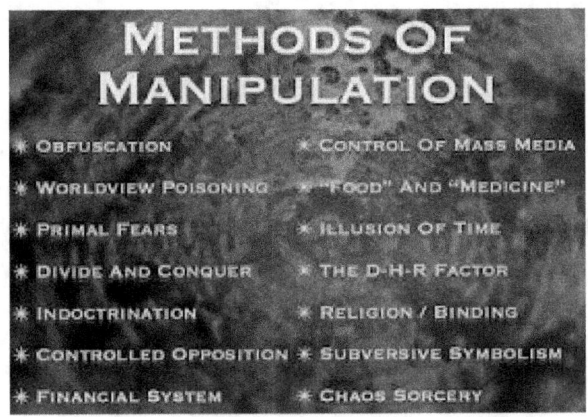

METHODS OF MANIPULATION

* OBFUSCATION	* CONTROL OF MASS MEDIA
* WORLDVIEW POISONING	* "FOOD" AND "MEDICINE"
* PRIMAL FEARS	* ILLUSION OF TIME
* DIVIDE AND CONQUER	* THE D-H-R FACTOR
* INDOCTRINATION	* RELIGION / BINDING
* CONTROLLED OPPOSITION	* SUBVERSIVE SYMBOLISM
* FINANCIAL SYSTEM	* CHAOS SORCERY

*(D-H-R = Denial – Harassment – Ridicule)

Crazy Al then slips into his grand finale of the Wizard of Oz on crack, in stating the following: "What occurred is that on December 21, 2012 a number of things happened. One is that the holographic timeline on which our collective travels shifted from a positive timeline, such that the plans and projects that were conceived on the catastrophic timeline, in what we call 'duality consciousness' (in what I call 'severe schizophrenia') of 'I win, you lose', no longer have traction now in the positive timeline of unity consciousness, (this is the most pathetic stab at 'We are the World', Zionists mouthpieces have ever attempted) which is 'we are one'. Somebody changed the video game (oh so now the New World Order is a video game in the matrix I suppose?). We're no longer in 'war, disease, crime and poverty', we're now in 'paradise on earth...'. I've have to give Crazy Al a 5 yard penalty on this **"decoy #4"** newspeak and translate its actual meaning as follows. Even though he and his pals he represents continue their highway robberies in the Federal Reserve, the stock market, human and heroin trafficking, international austerity and stolen oil, arms sales to terrorists and the mass dispersing of Palestinians and Syrians alike, no one is focusing on them anymore. His reference to "somebody changed the video game", once translated means that much thanks to their

183

other many contingency plans like the false-flag operations of the France and California "terrorist shootings", they have successfully diverted the masses' attention away from Newmerika's insiders' crimes and towards other stories such as "ISIS" (which they themselves created as a tool) and the Middle East. But make no mistake, the "catastrophic timeline" objectives, as Crazy Al prefers calling it, were still fully conducted in "perfect crimes" with undetected execution.

Also, one should not forget that Crazy Al has openly professed in his resume' to be an "expert in diffusion", though some might prefer a better choice of words, such as "confusion". Nonetheless, Crazy Al Webre has stolen a page from the "Ascension" or "Alien Saviors" playbook. He has premeditated to purposely sway the jury into a false sense of security by insinuating that we needn't concern ourselves with the NWO any longer, because "the light has already arrived". This is Marxist-Leninist poppycock in classical form and gets a "best in show" from me as **"decoy #5".** What it attempts to actually do is to "demotivate awakening people" from taking any action that actually would make a difference (such as forming their own political and monetary structures and domestic demonstrations).

It still baffles the senses that British and Newmerikan governments and institutions actually shell out big bucks to guys like Crazy Al, who all sound like they've just come from one of those MK Ultra drug experiments. And like the "Energizer Bunny", Al still continues to ramble on as follows: "Now, getting around to this..., what this means is that the controllers, the matrix, as part of their depopulation plan, had included a financial collapse component as sort of the centerpiece, or one of the centerpieces, of the depopulation plan that would click-in say around 2015. And if they could combine that with a World War Three, if they could combine that with famine, if they could combine that with Ebola and GMOs, hey, you know, its mass extinction. It's exterminate the surface dwellers. So it remains to be seen that the financial system is going to collapse in the usual expected way. Why? Because none of the false-flags have worked in the way that we think". (Sorry Crazy Al, but I've reserved the right for my own way of thinking, thank you).

And this brings things to **"decoy #6".** Though it has nothing to do with "positive timelines", the 9-11-like, evil depopulation plan and its associated false-flags it is true, will fail. Crazy Al Webre has been interpreted by others here, to have suffered from a Freudian slip when he mentions, "none of their false-flags has worked in the way we think". This context, "the way that we think" for a normal person is to not expect globalists to sabotage their own attacks, so in "throwing the game" they might not have worked "in the way that we think", but make no mistake (don't get your attention "diffused") they have served the purposes for which they were designed for. As for this scary campfire story propagandists are spreading about the whole "economic collapse" and depopulation campaigns, its intentions are designed to stampede the herd into the arms of the BRICS "saviors".

To differentiate between the decoy – NWO and the actual – NWO, let's put it into a "problem – reaction – solution" form of context:

Problem: The evil Anglosphere (actually, Marxist-Leninist puppeteers) are setting out to kill everyone and steal everything.

Reaction: Angry and fearful, the people long for putting an end to an old system and starting something new.

Solution: On white unicorns, angelic BRICS power elites swoop into action to save the day, by giving the world a new financial system and all the money people need.

Once again, Crazy Al Webre: "Right now, in kind of a 3-D perspective there are lots of forces that are jockeying, but right now what it appears to be is that it's not going to be a sudden collapse;

it's going to be a gradual transition. And what's occurring is that the Rothschild dollar sector is collapsing because of its own lawlessness, which it itself has induced. Whereas the BRICS sector is based on honored contracts, respect for individual and national sovereignty, and they're coming together by the two major gold producers in the world, around a gold-centered currency...,".

Crazy Al succeeds in attracting a whole swarm of referees on this play for **"decoy #7".** It is true that the transition will be gradual, but what Crazy Al's mind-screw left out is, the currency change will be due to the fact that the International Monetary Fund (IMF) in 1969, had already created the dollar's reserve currency replacement, the "SDR". Though the Rothschilds might be the "king daddy Zionists" of the heap, this fiasco isn't collapsing because of their lawlessness. An article in a 1988 "The Economist", an economic propaganda-rag magazine, partially owned by the Rothschilds themselves, even openly makes mention of replacing the U.S. dollar with a renamed SDR sometime around 2018.

I have concluded that Newmerikans now have two choices. They can awaken their awareness, share their proactive opinions peacefully and lawfully, push-back against the Marxist-Leninist mainstream politicians and media and actively participate for change, even if it means replacing 90% of its government. So it can do this, or it can do nothing. If the "do nothings" win the majority of the consensus, it will not be a pretty ending. As I have been quoted in the past, "democracy has no automatic pilot". You use it, participate in it, flood every one of your representatives', Congresspersons' and Senators' phone lines, emails, snail-mailboxes and fax machines with "your 2 cents" on all matters and issues which concern you. You "use it", or you will lose it.

To do nothing will only accelerate an approach of a very different horizon, blackened with divisions of marching storm troopers. I have personally studied history, past empires and the variable theories of the outcome in "doing nothing" under Newmerika's current conditions. Just as Vladimir Putin emulates, "never to forget" that people gave their lives, so that you might sit here, to do nothing you have insisted upon fate that it will now become necessary for the people to die yet again.

Chapter VI

An Historic Intervention

"The only thing necessary for the triumph of evil, is that good men do nothing", Edmund Burke. With Newmerikan's President Obama's state of appeal being in the slumps, against a backdrop of a 91% disapproval rating for Washington's Congress and Senate, it makes the status quo wonder just who is running their government? Certainly not its people.

Over the past decade it has been reported that over 12 million homes were illegally stolen by MERS mortgage fraud, while Associated Press reporters were harassed by the IRS for reporting "truth" in editorials, displeasing to the president.

As the National Defense Authorization Act (NDAA) was passed, a law permitting Newmerika's government to arrest people secretly and at whim, without due process or the right to a phone call and have them held indefinitely, Newmerika's people did nothing. Executive Order #13603 was passed giving sweeping powers for a President to act as "a king", whereby he can now seize everything you own (including your life) at the drop of a hat.

It has been reported that today people stand an 8x's greater chance of being accidently killed by their own police than by terrorists. Today the #1 cause of death in the military is "suicide". Luckily, alternative news media has become more successful in exposing the deluge in the "crimes of the affluent", yet the U.S. Congress just narrowly failed to curb online journalists and the rush is on to take control over the Newmerikan internet, much in the same fashion as the Zionist-Jewish Crime bosses have already accomplished with television networks. The failed attempt to curb journalists was led by Diane Feinstein and John McCain. Newmerika is at a moment in time where it is operating purely as a "liberal totalitarian State". With less than 10% of the people approving of a government who can make them disappear on a whim, with their military's #1 cause of death being suicide, what else in God's name can you call this? Certainly not "a democracy".

When more than 90% of a peoples walking around believing they hate their government, but do not express opposition in the name of "fear", or "distrusting their government", or because the government might bring them harm, then honey your "democracy" left the scene a long time ago; "it's gone"! Newmerikans now find themselves at the front stoops of a "Fascist Nation". Call it neglect, indifference, apathy, sheeple-phobia, fence-sitting, or whatever the causes. What it really boils down to is Newmerikans have been successfully taken control of without a shot needing to be fired and they will be leaving their children one great hell hole of a world to exist and survive in. When its principles have fallen to a foundation level based on fear, ass-licking and back-stabbing innuendo, it is the precursor to a Fascist State.

According to researcher Debra Tavares, people are already disappearing off the streets. She claims people are being quietly incarcerated and forcibly medicated against their will. No one though, seems to be exploring, or investigating her reports to verify their legitimacy. I tend to not be easily intimidated by fear. When one awards silence and indifference to the occult, one is greatly exaggerating any power which might or might not exist. Much like the "fear" of Dorothy's friends in the Wizard of Oz, her lion friend's fear is what gave the Wizard his power and not from any power he already had himself.

There's a famous quote by Martin Niemoller, a prominent Protestant pastor who spent 7 years in a Nazi concentration camp. It goes:

"First they came for the Socialists and I did not speak out –

Because I was not a Socialist.

Then they came for the Trade Unionists and I did not speak out –

Because I was not a Trade Unionist.

Then they came for the Jews and I did not speak out –

Because I was not a Jew.

Then they came for me – and there was no one left to speak for me".

I have never fully accepted the conspiracy theory of "secret entities" controlling or manipulating the weather, through a means known as HAARP. What is disturbing to me is the effects of climate change and how it might actually leapfrog the whole Fascist agenda. Enter, exhibit A: The researcher I recently referred to, Ms. Deborah Tavares who announced in a June, 2015 broadcast interview that California was resorting to some alarming extremes in dealing with water shortages. You should also keep in mind that this brings "a quadrupling effect into collision in California. It already behaving as a police State + a soon-to-be drought-causing exodus + the 150 year anniversary (2016-2017) of the California "Killer Quake" (the last one was 149 years ago and occurs about every 150 years) + the Fukushima radiation hush-up that's riddled its entire coastline.

Addressing the water issue, water resource shortages have now reached a point (according to Tavares) where "toilet-to-tap" water programs have been initiated. California has recently resorted to recycling its human waste water to tap water. In unisons, trailer loads of portable FEMA detention center cells have been quietly sighted late in 2015, making regular trips through Washington State, Montana, Idaho, Oregon and now California. Tavares also claims to have witnessed more public and open encouragement to migrate "out-of-California".

Though Taveres attributes all this to a New World Order type conspiracy, instigated by HAARP control to induce droughts, I beg to differ. That's what separates myself, a "realist" from Ms. Tavares, a "conspiracy theorist". FEMA is not as occult or conspiring as many of its critics like to assume. Let's face it, "there's a killer quake on the way". You see the quake is estimated to kill no less than 10,000 people in and around Los Angeles alone. That means 100's of thousands of people will be without power and sewer services for up to a year. It also means they'll have an abnormally high amount of looters and vandals to lock up. So it only stands to reason that the federal government could easily just be preparing for that with its portable FEMA cells. Furthermore, the drought in question has no doubt happened before in history. It only gets reported with hysteria when it affects millions of people.

It was once said that during the early 1600's the Europeans kicked out all their religious fanatics, so they fled to the U.S. where they proceeded to burn women at the stake for being witches. And it has also been said that the "Elite-criminal Jews" were kicked out of Russia and also fled to the U.S. where they became bankers, funders of terrorism and promoters of new world order-like agendas and policies. It is a twist in historic irony that Newmerika now finds itself slipping farther and farther back to the ways of the old USSR, while the new Russia becomes more and more as a pre-Kennedy assassination America used to be.

It is said that Newmerikans lost their freedom through a series of psychological techniques intended to brainwash and promote that the concepts of "scheming", "trickery" and "questioning government" were cast in a light of being unpatriotic, of dissidence, too foolish and ridiculous to be considered or associated with the establishment. With only 6 corporations controlling 90% of the U.S, media, this now makes it a daunting task to live in Newmerika without experiencing a poisoning of the mind. GE, Newscorp, Disney, Viacom, Time Warner and CBS. Since 1983 some 50 different companies have now been consolidated down to these six who pretty much control everything Newmerikans read, watch and listen to. These entities are interrelated with big oil, the Industrial Military Complex, Wall Street, the Federal Reserve and Israel. Through campaign finances they control who gets elected, while by whatever means of programming is deemed necessary, be it subliminal or otherwise, they see to it that Newmerikans remain willing slaves, accepting of their serfdom.

On March 27thth, 2015 the Department of Homeland Security's Special Operations Forces practiced "political dissent extraction" drills in Fort Lauderdale, Florida. Texas Governor Greg Abbott was outraged at the "Jade Helm" maneuvers taking place in his State. He not being consulted beforehand, nor included in any specifics as to what they were for, ordered his State National Guard to monitor its activities.

Texas resident Travis Kuenstler took photos with crystal clarity of 3 missiles mounted at 45 degree angles, about 45 miles southeast of Lubbock, Texas. They appeared to be about 25 to 30 feet in length, known as SAM missiles and were said by officials, "not to exist" and are rumored to be connected to some sort of WWIII strategy. However, with the compiling amount of false-flag activity already committed by the Newmerikan regime, I can't decipher if these missiles are intended for a foreign enemy, or to be targeted domestically.

Behavioral modification is used in conjunction with Newmerikan media, much like the Russian psychologist Ivan Pavlov first used with dogs (hence "Pavlov's dog"). The technique is known as Classic Conditioning. Most of Newmerikans' minds will now denigrate anything sounding in association with a "conspiracy theory". This is largely evident in the terrorist-like treatment of Newmerika's heroes who expose malice and corruption in government, only to be swiftly marginalized and branded a "conspiracy theorist" or "whistleblower".

Another Newmerikan mainstream media procedure performed was first publicized by B.F. Skinner, known as "Behavioral Modification", based on "Operant Conditioning". It is performed through changing environmental events as they related to a person's behavior and beliefs. Behavioral modification both instigates and reinforces any theory of conspiracy to become "fallacy", while it is mixed with the operant conditioning. This correlates into conjunction with creating a false paradigm, or as the Nazis used to say, "Tell a lie long enough, until it becomes true".

So with Classic Conditioning, Operant Conditioning and Behavioral Modification comes "Normalcy Bias". It is the end product of all three conditioning techniques which permeate the "belief systems" of Newmerikans. Before the advent of television had Fast and Furious, Jade Helm, Benghazi, the NSA scandal, the Federal Reserve's "Fractional Reserve Banking" (where it creates 10 dollars out of one to loan out), it would have sent millions into the streets in protest and demonstrations. But with the psycho-manipulation of T.V. viewers' minds, Newmerika's sheeples will prefer to remain glued to the sofa while the elitists, wizards of high crimes and misdemeanors can continue their lives with uninterrupted, perfect crimes.

Normalcy Bias is actually responsible for "crisis style management" in Newmerika, whereby people wait for a crisis before addressing the issue. The U.S. government debt being a perfect example. I know for myself, I couldn't fully come to terms with this sickness until finally I kicked it by not watching television for five years running now. I do confide to watching RT and CCTV. Those and only online alternative news, renting movies and buying lots more books to read.

Being well known to psychologists and sociologists, Normalcy Bias is experienced in times of facing disasters or impending dangers where its victims enter a mental state of denial. Not only are the possible consequences of an oncoming danger to their health and safety minimized, but the onset of catastrophic conditions becomes underestimated as well. The condition remains psychotic within the individual throughout each day, so long as they are getting their daily dose of T.V. programming. Normalcy Bias instills in people a false sense that since something has never happened before, it is likely not to ever occur.

As is with a baby and its blanket, the subjects cling to their habitual, repetitive, daily routines regardless of any overwhelming evidence that danger lies ahead. An example of this in action would be watching the many dissident extractions and martial law drills, such as Jade Helm, which are being quietly implemented routinely by the sitting president, without any investigative or open questioning of these in-the-dark maneuvers.

One of Normalcy Bias's most prominent side-effects are the inhibition of one's ability to prevent and cope with disaster, once it has arrived. Its victims experience great difficulties in reacting to any incidental situations which have never occurred before. Normalcy Bias tends to lure its victims through the subconscious, to interpret warnings and inaccurately reframes information. It facilitates projections of optimism which accompanies its subjects to a degree of perception that interprets a less serious nature. It numbs a person's oversight, quite similar to a pain-killing drug. If the California water crisis, Jade Helm, Edward Snowden's treatment, the U.S. budget deficit, the USS Liberty incident, Israel's encroachment and its human trafficking of 100's of thousands of East European girls into the sex slave trade, Hillary Clinton's Benghazi debacle and U.S. soldiers protecting someone's opium poppy fields in Afghanistan are seen by you (if you are a Newmerikan) as of no real concern, then you are likely a victim of Normalcy Bias.

"Learned Helplessness" was discovered by psychologist Martin Seligman and was observed when an animal put on an electric grid was repeatedly subjected to annoying or aversive stimulus which it could not escape. Over time the animal would stop trying to avoid the stimulus and lay down to accept the change as being helpless. The real twist to this discovery showed that over time, even when offered opportunities to escape were introduced, the psychosis prevented the animal from doing so.

Just as Seligman's dog on the electric grid demonstrated this affliction, so does Newmerika's daily citizenry. Even when faced with glaring, overwhelming evidence of authentic criminality is being done by bankers, politicians, or Israel, Newmerika has been conditioned not to act, "especially if they are Zionist Jews". It lays down to accept drinking waste-water, criminality in government, mortgage theft, a murdered president, the concept of dissidents, intrusive surveillance, overly perverted and graphic entertainment and the list goes on.

Newmerikans have given up, they've surrendered. They have been so conditioned and mentally tenderized to convince themselves that in the unresponsiveness to their demand they believe that their actions will never have any effect. They are existing in a world as life on an imprisoned planet. Though Newmerikans actually still do possess the ability to bring about change, they must take the first step by repelling intimidation. Even in a democracy "change" takes more than just voting or writing somebody a check.

The profound, bought-and-paid-for apathy of Newmerikans politicians should not be permitted to cloud their focus in what they expect their representatives to achieve for them. Since Newmerika's are being subjugated into perceiving they don't make a difference, by the means of mental media conditioning, then its past time to recoup their truer identities by deflecting the controls back at their T.V.s and start taking the necessary steps to greatly alter how they use them and how they live their lives. Their present standing in current times have them embedded in a deep rut made by the wheel of their corporate media controllers, making them primed to accept anything, consciously or unconsciously, which their government does or does not do.

It is said that "depopulation" will be the end result of Newmerikans passivity. A unified effort within the more truthful alternative media remains their last, brightening glimmer of hope. If not soon actively utilized, Newmerika is destined to become a nation consisting of people willingly conditioned to walk into the furnaces of death camps. In the words of Howard Beale, "Turn off your T.V.s"! (Read books, make noise).

"Zero T.V." households is what sends programming networks and mind controllers spinning their wheels off and going into panic attacks. As more people turn their backs on the big service providers, cable and satellite T.V. service is falling by the wayside. Zero T.V. households are now comprised of some 6 million non-viewers, up from 2 million in 2007 according to the Nielsen Corporation. In a mad scramble broadcasters are trying to figure out how to win them back, as more people begin ditching their T.V. service. At a National Association of Broadcasters' (NAB) show, broadcasters discussed ways to keep cable and satellite customers under their control, at the Las Vegas annual meeting.

In an urgency to adapt to a new generation, big broadcaster are trying to come up with more "pay-for-programs-you-like" and "watch-when-you-want" type gimmicks, to meet the new generation where it is. Dennis Wharton, spokesman for NAB says "Getting broadcast programs on all the gizmos and gadgets – like tablets, laptops and the backseat cars is highly important". In another act of desperation to win back customers, T.V. ratings giant Nielsen plans to measure T.V. viewing quarterly. They intend to utilize the results to recalculate how ads are displayed, in the hopes of recouping a generation that is turning away from cable and satellite services.

Cheaper online video subscriptions like Netflix and Amazon cost less than $15 a month combined and are making video choices more accessible.

Reports indicate that those going without service tends to be younger, single and without children. Dounin Turrill, Nielsen's Senior Vice President of Insights says that part of the new monitoring regime is meant to help in determining whether the young generation will change their behavior over time. The major broadcasters seem to be in a panic, looking for new ways to utilize their mind control machines. Since the ease of the internet, new generations are looking elsewhere for their information and entertainment. Only 46,000 of the 974,000 households created in 2012, signed up as T.V. service customers, according to research form SNL Kagan.

Since the advent of T.V. popularity in the 1950's, after more than 65 years, we are finally witnessing less and less and less minds controlled no more. The demographics are changing and broadcasters know this, so they remain cautious. Can they adapt to an ever changing culture to once recapture their thoughts, so far remains a futile challenge.

No, potential T.V. viewers don't feel their missing out on anything anymore, since they've a newfound attitude which makes them wary of 24 news channels, or the latest MTV buzz based on gossip. They no longer have to resort to flipping channels, or waiting for something that's been targeted at them. Frankly speaking, there doesn't seem to be anything that will bring them back to traditional viewing when they can still find more authentic and unbiased stuff online, through their devices "for free".

New no-T.V.'ers say they don't want someone dictating to them what media they'll be watching. And what's more, they don't report ever experiencing any peer pressure for these decisions. They flat out say, "I feel less in control of what's being reflected to me when I have T.V". So far, there seems to be three growing trends big broadcasters are scrambling to analyze. They are "cable cutters", "cable shavers" and "cord nevers". The cutters have cast away the concept of paying for T.V. altogether. The shavers are trying to save money by reducing the number of channels and T.V.s they have in the home. We should keep in mind, certain immigrants often fall into this slot, favoring only Hispanic, Asian, or Hindi programming. As for cord-nevers, they're usually the youngest users who totally embrace smartphones, Netflix and/or internet alternatives, who never set-up landline services.

Taking charge of your own mind is the start to a happier, healthier outlook on life. Even if the alternative venues you've located bring you bad news sometimes, at least they offer an immense release of stress and burden knowing that you've been more informed of the truth. Releasing one's self from the double-speak and double-think of living lie after propagandizing lie is an historic intervention made by a brave new generation who's slamming the brakes on the old guards of mind control and new world order agendas, with bold statements like, "take this tube and shove it". I would however, like to stipulate one last measure of caution and that is, when it comes down to using Facebook "be forewarned", they're in bed with the U.S. Department of Defense, they "have admitted" to using mind-control tactics with them already, they have many Tavistock cronies and are situated right alongside your buddies at the Stanford Research Institute!

Chapter VII

Piece by Piece

One of the many admired attributes of Vladimir Putin is that, though however pragmatic and calculating, he nonetheless throws heart and soul into his actions and never refuses or avoids taking ownership of his responsibilities, no matter the odds. Being a shining example as a boy, much like Genghis Khan, who was born into a very simple life, once he found himself he diligently remained focused to his virtuous ideals and ambitions, pulling himself up by the bootstraps and his entire nation along with him, using only what God had given both himself and his peoples.

Leaving not one nook or cranny unturned or gone to waste, he was and is his own man. With vast reservoirs of patience, generosity, compassion, energy and stamina he remains ardent to the foundational principles of his culture, which makes Russia so tastefully rich. Though some might be inclined to say, "He was only doing his job" he has proven through this day to leave that phrase's words in the dust. He has done this by not only being a man of his word, but one who takes time to consider fully, the environments around him. Acting always from a standpoint of dedication, once executed, both his actions and his accomplishments quickly standout with a noticeable brand of quality that is all his own and a cut above the rest.

Yes he is a lawyer, a politician and a president, but he has never denied himself to also be a father, adventurer, athlete, marksman, pilot, horseback rider, racecar driver, hiker, climber, hang-glider, hunter, fisherman, biker, environmentalist, animal lover, worker and most of all "a real man" and human being. What the Americans failed to learn about Kennedy is what the Russian people must never forget. Even one great man who is his own man in his own right, is reliant upon the support of his people. Take that away and all that any great men have done, will be in vain. Just as in a democracy, in living life there is no automatic pilot. All things, no matter how pleasurable, require periodic intervals of maintenance, gratitude, respect, reassessment, support and question.

It is no longer the world's secret that the same beast challenging President Putin today is one-in-the-same beast who seeks to control America's people. The Zionist puppeteers in their Israeli colony known as America are hell-bent in their lusts and their last throws to dominate and control all peoples and all things, in a thick atmosphere full of blood and total disregard. Much thanks to Vladimir Putin's persistent dedication and the ever-awakening Western peoples, this beast is soon to drop its sword and go home. In a last angst of desperation it will attempt to devour its own people.

The world will sentence Newmerika' to solitary confinement and President Putin and his people will inherit what the Newmerikans lost more than 50 years ago. If Newmerikans are smart enough, spread and share their awareness and forge an impenetrable unity, they might have a chance at reducing that sentence in isolationism that is quickly coming upon them. What it will require is to target, expose, connect all the dots, "arrest", "prosecute" and "jail" without fines or slaps of the wrist, all members of their establishment who are attempting to bring the entire world to the floors of hell in an Armageddon.

Picture a pyramid being disassembled piece by piece and as it is being done very bright lights are shown in every hidden room, every closet and each corner. This is what it would require to transform Newmerika back into America. The careful extraction of every Tavistock mole inside the Mossad and the CIA because these institutions are not bad when freely conducted as they were intended to be, but they are now only controlled by very bad people. And to all Europeans, please read my lips; "you are all being made the doormat-of-death by these very same evil constituents"! Do something about it. Wake up, smell the coffee and do not become the sacrificial lamb to the first and last nuclear war!

"Sanction back"! By this I mean to sanction Russia is to sanction yourselves, Newmerikans included. Newmerikans, Europeans the Russians and Chinese, we all share the same enemy and he is none of us. "Sanction back" and sever all associations with anything or anybody connected to the following entities:

Freemasons, Tavistock Institute, Human Relations Journal, U.S. media networks, Clear Channel, The Evaluation Journal, University of Sussex, Facebook, Esalen, MIT, Hudson Insitute, The Heritage Foundation, Georgetown University, U.S. Airforce and Naval Intelligence, Mount Pelerin Society, Trilateral Commission, Bilderberg member corporations and their products, Ditchley Foundation, Club of Rome, Harvard University, SHAEF, American Jewish Congress, US Commission on Community Relations, US National Education Association, Newmerika's New Foreign Policy Initiative, U.S. Institute of Social Research and Training Lab, Wharton School, Any Warburg groups, Sandoz AG, Human Ecology Fund, U.S. Institute for Foreign Studies, Ford Foundation, U.S. Students for a Democratic Society, Hoover Institute, Bechtel Group, Kaiser, APEC, Rockefeller Foundation, U.S. Counsel on Foreign

Relations, Brooking Institute, Skull and Crossbones, Freedom House, U.S. Federal Reserve, Peabody Fund, John Slater Fund, Carnegie Institution, any Carnegie endowments, Russell Sage Foundation, American International Corporation, U.S. National Institute of Health, Flow Laboratories, Merle Thomas Corporation, Walden Research, Planning Research Corporation, Arthur D. Little, General Electric, TEMPO, Operations Research Inc., NTL Institute for Applied Behavioral Sciences, Western Training Laboratories of Group Development, U.S. Institute for the Future, Simplot Corporation, The League for Industrial Democracy, Samuel Rubin Foundation, Stern Family Fund, National and World Council of Churches, Charles F. Kettering Foundation, Wells Fargo Bank, Hewlett Packard, Bank of America, McDonald Douglas, Blyth, Eastman Dillion, TRW, RAND Corporation, UCLA, American Management Association, GTE, Sylvania, AT&T, Chase Bank, IBM, Uniform Law Foundation, Mellon Bank and Facebook.

The above entities are guilty of one or more of the following: being anti-sovereign, anti-democratic, anti-small business, anti-freedom, pro-corruption, pro-mind control and/or pro-Tavistock. The largest associations of all the above mentioned entities have been directly related to "mind-control" experimentations and have close associations with the Tavistock Institute.

Today the Tavistock Institute syphons off more than $9 billion annually of U.S. taxpayer revenues. Once you become aware of the true objective of these foundations and agencies, it no longer remains a mystery why interest rates rise along with higher taxes, the destabilization of the family unit occurring, the devaluation of churches sliding into forums for revolutions, the digression of universities turning into overly monitored, CIA drug addiction cesspools, or why chambers of government transform into toxic halls for international espionage and corrupt lobbying.

They are in direct violation of their charters by issuing grants only to causes which serve specific political agendas. Many of these foundations illegally employ professional intelligence operatives, "not charitable workers", to serve sinister, political and socio-economic goals.

Having been granted "tax exemption", the foundations in question commit tax fraud on a daily basis, as well as "criminal syndication" and conspiracy against the United States of America, under Constitutional Law 213, Corpus Juris Secundum 16. This is not conspiracy theory, this is very authentic criminality and I personally would consider them to be "enemies of the State" and certainly of all U.S. citizens.

As I made mention earlier, Vladimir Putin is first a man of caution and of pragmatism. Yes, he is a doer and a man of action, but he always remains wise to first consider his environment and the repercussions of his actions. This often runs counter to a West that is always running its mouth off half-cocked. If you are a Newmerikan reading this then you must realize that the same entities sanctioning his nation are also sanctioning you. The same sabre-rattlers attempting to control him are the same people trying to control you.

America is a failed past and Russia is a rising future. America has been fully pillaged by a very vulgar, indecent, severely deranged and rapacious bourgeoisie. It has become a nation operated by authorities who have gone out of their minds in trying to control other's minds. Its ruling class has opened the prelude to its death kneel, in the epitome of berserk sin. The makeup of their consistency was born from overly in-bred families whose deficiencies and foul blood were first revealed by Genghis Khan. He proved that a dirt-poor, half starving goat shepherd boy could not only rise to become the greatest ruler in all the world, but also the father of commerce, regulated currency, international trade, engineering, inventory control, the post office, retirement planning, strategic defense, collaboration and coexistence.

He conquered the very forefathers of the deviant minions who now attempt to conquer you. He proved to them openly and glaringly that "regulated, selective breeding" was a complete and utter sham. When one compares what he contributed to humanity to what has been accomplished by these frustrated psychopaths in the West's leadership, other than technology, they haven't been able to advance civilization one inch!

They are still riding on the same inventions and innovations founded by a man from over 800 years ago. They have earned no privileges and they are not deserving of any exclusive rights, including the right to eliminate your rights and the right to a voice in choosing "peace with Russia" and open trade, and not some cockamamie, lying and orchestrated reason to do the opposite, just to keep feeding a Defense Department with a bottomless pit! The current leadership in NATO, Newmerika and the disassembling Europe are their own people's worst enemy because they are everybody's enemy; they have no friends! Take a look around the world and tell me what you see. They have no friends. And they have only destroyed civilization and they have contributed absolutely nothing to enhance it.

They loathe anyone who stands for peace, truthfulness, justice and respectful coexistence. And they especially loathe Vladimir Putin because "this is a man"!

www.ingramcontent.com/pod-product-compliance
Lightning Source LLC
Chambersburg PA
CBHW071343280526
45787CB00001B/205